D0289154

Having received the highest level of education in both medicine and ministry, Carol Peters-Tanksley is rightfully a physician of the body and soul. Her knowledge of the Bible and medical science refracted through the prism of her extended experience as a medical doctor and minister is reflected on these pages in a most helpful way. Her goal is to minister healing and wholeness to individuals who deal in one way or another with anxiety and fear. There is biblical wisdom, spiritual insights, and practical advice in this volume. Written in simple and straightforward language and avoiding unnecessary clinical and theological vocabulary, this book offers insights, illumination, and spiritual direction to both casual and sophisticated readers. I am happy to highly recommend it to anyone desiring healing, wholeness, and a life of righteousness, peace, and joy in the Holy Spirit.

—Thomson K. Mathew, DMin, EdD
Professor of Pastoral Care and Former Dean, College of
Theology and Ministry, Oral Roberts University

I am pleased to endorse Dr. Carol Peters-Tanksley's latest book, *Overcoming Fear and Anxiety Through Spiritual Warfare*. Dr. Peters-Tanksley provides sound mental health and spiritual advice concerning one of the most common mental health and spiritual challenges evidenced today: anxiety. Her description of the many aspects of life that contribute to fear and anxiety is clear and easily understood. The suggestions she makes regarding ways to overcome anxiety are clearly in line with principles of good mental health. Most importantly her approaches to overcoming the spiritual aspects of anxiety are sound and biblically based. She describes spiritual warfare and the processes involved in overcoming the "slings and arrows" of life in language that confirms the love of God, the grace of Christ, and the presence of the Holy Spirit as available to everyone who is in distress. Dr. Peters-Tanksley truly believes, as do I, that God does not desire any of His children to be bound by fear or anxiety. .

—Edward E. Decker Jr., PhD
Retired Professor and Chair of Christian Counseling
Graduate School of Theology and Ministry
Oral Roberts University

Have you ever seen two things that seem diametrically opposed yet true at the same time? Some call it a paradox. Others call it both/and instead of either/or. My friend Carol Peters-Tanksley will take you on that journey in *Overcoming Fear and Anxiety Through Spiritual Warfare*. Instead of your feeling guilty and ashamed of fear and anxiety as a Christian, Dr. Carol will teach you to have faith and confidence in the middle of your challenges. This book will challenge and empower you to live confident and unafraid.

—Sam Chand
Leadership Consultant and Author, *Leadership Pain*

Overcoming Fear and Anxiety Through Spiritual Warfare by Dr. Carol Peters-Tanksley is one of the most valuable and well-written resources on mental health, fear, and anxiety that I have come across. I recommend this book for pastors, educators, mental health workers, those in the helping professions, and anyone who has struggled with fear or anxiety. [As someone who has faced sexual abuse, chronic illness, long-term caregiving, and other stress-related issues, I found Dr. Peters-Tanksley's approach to be refreshingly insightful, comprehensive, and compassionate while remaining biblically and medically sound.]

↲ —Shelly Beach
Cofounder, PTSD Perspectives
Award-Winning Author, *The Silent Seduction of Self-Talk*

Dr. Carol's book offers the reader a unique approach to spiritual warfare with a focus on fear and anxiety. In a reader-friendly style the author combines medical science with her practical/personal/ministry experience, resulting in an understandable guide. While there are many books and articles on spiritual warfare, Dr. Carol applies these principles in a practical and refreshing way. When faced with difficulty, readers can apply biblical self-examination, deal with anything revealed appropriating Jesus's healing, and finally stand in the full understanding of biblical truth. Dr. Carol reminds us of our love relationship with "God the Father," which takes us into His presence with healing, freedom, and authority in Christ. Dr. Carol takes us on a fresh journey to becoming that new creature in Christ, free of anxiety and fear. I have no doubt that God through His Holy Spirit will speak to you through this book.

—Donald R. Tredway, MD, PhD
Former Chairman, Department of Obstetrics & Gynecology
for Oral Roberts University School of Medicine and the
University of Oklahoma Tulsa Medical College
Founder, Resurrection Ministries

Speaking from her unique vantage point of theological and clinical integration, Dr. Carol addresses the important yet controversial topic of spiritual warfare with sensitivity and insight. Her realistic perspective and holistic approach lend themselves to a fresh and helpful understanding of the interaction between human experience and spiritual forces. I especially value the manner in which Dr. Carol dispels magical notions of spiritual warfare by emphasizing the practical strategies by which God works by His Spirit within the human heart. I heartily recommend this book for anyone seeking to effectively address experiences of fear and anxiety.

—Bill Buker, DMin, PhD, LPC
Professor of Christian Counseling, Graduate School of
Theology and Ministry, Oral Roberts University

In her newest book, *Overcoming Fear and Anxiety Through Spiritual Warfare*, Dr. Carol combines her medical expertise with a biblical perspective to provide wise practical Christian counsel for effectively dealing with the complex and universal problems of fear and anxiety. She understands the interweaving of the spirit-mind-body connections and how each affects the others. Dr. Carol stirs hope and assurance that you can be an overcomer!

—Paul L. King, ThD, DMin
Pastor, Professor, Author of Eleven Books, Including *God's Healing Arsenal* and *Creating a Healing Community*

Overcoming Fear and Anxiety Through Spiritual Warfare boldly confronts the tools that are used to rob many people of the life God intended for them. Through Scripture, her knowledge, and her experience Carol teaches readers how to recognize these mind-sets in their own lives. She provides practical steps to free themselves and get on course with the plan God has for each of us.

—Joe Champion
Senior Pastor, Celebration Church, Austin, Texas
Member, Board of Reference, Oral Roberts University

From the moment I met Dr. Carol Peters-Tanksley, I felt as if I had known her for years! Her warmth and presence as she communicates in person are duplicated beautifully in her latest book, *Overcoming Fear and Anxiety Through Spiritual Warfare*. Like she is, the book is refreshingly balanced and totally uncondemning, and her scrutiny of fear and anxiety is engaging and practical from start to finish! Nothing is left untouched, no stone is left unturned in her quest to lead you on the path to healing. Her medical and ministry experience allows her to weave a thorough examination of the possible physical, emotional, and spiritual causes of fear and anxiety. Then she devotes great energy to offering practical, down-to-earth steps toward freedom with the confidence of someone who has done it well!

—Jane Evans
Senior Pastor, Influencers Church Global
Director, bU Women's Conferences

No one is exempt from fear and anxiety, especially in today's world. In this book Dr. Carol unpacks the common causes and offers powerful, practical, and possible solutions for overcoming. By understanding the enemy's strategies and their identity in Christ, along with the *power* behind their words, worship, prayer, and Christian community, readers will learn *practical* ways to apply this knowledge in their daily lives. Yes, it is *possible* to ensure the enemy's defeat and be confident and unafraid! Dr. Carol's spiritual warfare strategies are not just a list of Christian to-dos that depend on the reader's own efforts. Her strategies are a natural outcome of God's grace working in the hearts of all believers as they grow in intimacy with the living Christ.

—Mary J. Nelson
Pastor of Prayer and Author, *Jehovah-Rapha: The God Who Heals* and *Praying for the Cure*

Sometimes a clear voice is needed to navigate the basic pathways of life. The voice needs to have experience, education, and a solid understanding of God's Word and how to apply it to life. It isn't enough to know you have a problem; you need to know why you have a problem. What life experience brought this about? Knowing how to dig into the past so it can be corrected, or sanctified, takes a qualified guide. Dr. Carol is your guide. Enjoy the read. Enjoy the outcome.

—Rev. Dr. Howard S. Russell
President and CEO, Christian Healthcare Ministries

OVERCOMING

FEAR &
ANXIETY

THROUGH

SPIRITUAL WARFARE

CAROL PETERS-TANKSLEY, MD, DMIN

SILOAM

Most CHARISMA HOUSE BOOK GROUP products are available at special quantity discounts for bulk purchase for sales promotions, premiums, fund-raising, and educational needs. For details, write Charisma House Book Group, 600 Rinehart Road, Lake Mary, Florida 32746, or telephone (407) 333-0600.

OVERCOMING FEAR AND ANXIETY THROUGH SPIRITUAL WARFARE
    by Carol Peters-Tanksley
Published by Siloam
Charisma Media/Charisma House Book Group
600 Rinehart Road
Lake Mary, Florida 32746
www.charismahouse.com

Unless otherwise noted, all Scripture quotations are taken from the Modern English Version. Copyright © 2014 by Military Bible Association. Used by permission. All rights reserved.

Scripture quotations marked KJV are from the King James Version of the Bible.

Scripture quotations marked NIV are taken from the Holy Bible, New International Version®, NIV®. Copyright © 1973, 1978, 1984, 2011 by Biblica, Inc.™ Used by permission of Zondervan. All rights reserved worldwide. www.zondervan.com. The "NIV" and "New International Version" are trademarks registered in the United States Patent and Trademark Office by Biblica, Inc.™

Scripture quotations marked NKJV are taken from the New King James Version®. Copyright © 1982 by Thomas Nelson. Used by permission. All rights reserved.

Author's note: All italics in Scripture reflect the author's emphasis.

Cover design by Lisa Rae McClure
Design Director: Justin Evans

Visit the author's website at www.drcarolministries.com.

Library of Congress Cataloging-in-Publication Data:
An application to register this book for cataloging has been submitted to
the Library of Congress.
International Standard Book Number: 978-1-62999-097-2
E-book ISBN: 978-1-62999-098-9

17 18 19 20 21 — 9 8 7 6 5 4 3 2 1
Printed in the United States of America

To Wil,
For being the Christ–light to me
during my own journey out of fear
and anxiety and toward wholeness

CONTENTS

ACKNOWLEDGMENTS

THE GESTATION PERIOD is longer for some books than others. This specific one has been in the making for nearly ten years. Looking at the many individuals who have helped bring this book into being leaves me with a profound sense of gratitude.

First, I want to thank the doctor of ministry program at Oral Roberts University. During my time in that program I carried out much of the foundational study and research underlying the concepts in this book.[1] I must give special thanks to the program director, Dr. Kenneth Mayton, for your wisdom; my supervisor, Dr. Ed Decker, for consistently challenging me; and Dr. Thomson Mathew, then dean of the School of Theology and Missions, for your gracious support and unparalleled example of Christian excellence. And thank you to the entire faculty; your guidance allowed the seeds of this project to grow into something of value, and your investment in me as a person did much to help me develop into the professional I am now.

Thank you to Pastor Henry Adams and the congregation of Believers Christian Center, where a portion of this material was first presented. Your gracious welcome and honest feedback blessed me and made this material better.

A big thank-you to Ann Byle, my literary agent, for helping me keep things in perspective during difficult days and encouraging me when I needed it. And thank you to Tim Beals and Credo Communications for your continuing influence in my journey as a published author.

Thank you to Maureen Eha, my editor at Charisma House, for imagining what this book could be and having faith that I could write it. Your encouragement and experienced guidance have made this book so much better than it ever would have been without you. And thank you to the others at Charisma House who have been indispensable in bringing this book to life, especially Megan Turner, Ann Mulchan, and Debbie Marrie.

A loving thank-you to my husband, Al Tanksley, who passed away just before the actual writing of this book began. Even now you are, and you always will be, the wind beneath my wings. Your belief in me has given me strength to carry on and bring this message to those who need it. And I so look forward to seeing you again soon, when there will be no more tears, no more fear, no more anxiety, and no more death.

In a deeper and very important sense this book is a product of the person God has been growing me into during the past twenty-five years and of the many people He has used to help Him in that challenging process. Thanking them would take up a chapter in itself, but this book would never have come into being without the mentors, friends, professional helpers, pastors, and others who spoke into my life and were there during the times I myself struggled to hold on to hope. Your legacy in part lives on through the lives this book will touch.

Most of all, thank You to Jesus, my friend and Savior, for taking my brokenness and turning it into something nourishing that can feed and bless others. It is because of You that I can share my own testimony of overcoming. May Your love and grace use these pages to bring hope, healing, freedom, victory, and transformation to the men and women who read them.

INTRODUCTION

ICE ADMIRAL JAMES B. Stockdale was an officer in the US Navy during the Vietnam War. He became a fighter pilot, and in 1965 he was shot down while returning from his second combat tour over North Vietnam. Held for eight years as a prisoner of war (POW) in the "Hanoi Hilton," he suffered repeated torture and endured long periods of time in solitary confinement without any prisoner's rights and with no assurance that he would survive the war or live to see his family again.[1]

As the highest-ranking officer in the prison camp, Stockdale shouldered responsibility for the other men held there. He made it his mission to do everything in his power to help the men survive unbroken while at the same time leading the American resistance against Vietnamese attempts to use the prisoners for propaganda.[2] He instituted a cohesive set of rules governing prisoner behavior,[3] providing the men with hope and empowering them. He developed an elaborate method of internal communication the men could use even during enforced silence or solitary confinement.[4] Risking further torture or death if discovered, he found ways to forward secret intelligence to the US government through letters he was allowed to write to his wife. Following his release he received a total of twenty-six medals, including the Medal of Honor.

What kept Vice Admiral Stockdale sane during those years of imprisonment and torture? What allowed him to do so much to help many other men survive unbroken? Researcher and author Jim Collins writes of an enlightening conversation he had with Stockdale. When Collins asked how he made it through, Stockdale responded, "I never lost faith in the end of the story....I never doubted not only that I would get out, but also that I would prevail in the end and turn the experience into the defining event of my life, which, in retrospect, I would not trade."[2]

But not everyone made it through intact. Who didn't survive? The optimists. "They were the ones who said, 'We're going to be out by Christmas.' And Christmas would come, and Christmas would go. Then they'd say, 'We're going to be out by Easter.' And Easter would come, and Easter would go. And then Thanksgiving, and then it would be Christmas again. And they died of a broken heart."[3]

And then Stockdale told Collins the bottom line: "This is a very important lesson. You must never confuse faith that you will prevail in the end—which you can never afford to lose—with the discipline to confront the most brutal facts of your current reality, whatever they might be."[4]

That lesson has become known as the Stockdale paradox; "Retain faith that you will prevail in the end regardless of the difficulties, *and at the same time* confront the most brutal facts of your current reality, whatever they may be."[5]

You and I are also in a war. No, we're not flying fighter jets over North Vietnam. We're not chained with leg irons or held in solitary confinement. We don't have to communicate with central command through secret codes hidden in written letters. But we are in a war nonetheless.

If you've made a decision to follow Jesus and taken your stand on God's side, then you have an enemy. That enemy is not your inconsiderate and demanding boss, your trouble-making children, or your spouse, who knows just how to push your buttons. Your enemy is God's enemy—Satan and his kingdom of darkness. Although we do not see the enemy with our physical eyes, he is out to destroy us with more tenacity than any North Vietnamese army fighting against the US forces.

We may not think our fear and anxiety are part of the war between good and evil, God and Satan, but they are. Your psychological distress may be the result of physical vulnerabilities, outside circumstances, or lifestyle challenges, but it is still preventing you from experiencing God's best and from being effective for God's kingdom to the degree He needs you to be. Or it may be that your problems stem more directly from this war between God and Satan and are a result of specific attacks from the enemy.

Whatever the details, if you are living with fear and anxiety, you picked up this book hoping to find a path to freedom. And that path to freedom is the Stockdale paradox—looking at the factors involved in your psychological distress, including spiritual warfare, with brutal honesty while at the same time developing absolute faith in the freedom and victory Jesus makes available to you both now and in eternity.

During his captivity Vice Admiral Stockdale did not spend his energy blaming US government policy for ineffective execution of the war, as ineffective as those policies were. He didn't rail against his captors for their brutality, wallow in self-pity, or let fear make decisions for him. Yes, he had plenty of reasons to be anxious and afraid, but he focused his energy on surviving, resisting, and helping others. You too must focus your energy not on blaming others or wallowing in self-pity, but on surviving, resisting, and then helping others.

This book will help you work through the Stockdale paradox as it relates to your fear and anxiety. It will help you take an honest though perhaps uncomfortable look at your life right now. It will help you face the realities that may be contributing to your psychological distress, be they physical, mental, circumstantial, lifestyle related, or spiritual. It will help you confront the brutal facts about your vulnerabilities, including your own contribution to your distress. And it will help you see the many places where you can make changes that will help you lessen your distress.

And this book will help to grow your faith in the absolute certainty of victory—both now and in the end. It will help you understand what Christ's victory on the cross means for you when it comes to fear and anxiety and how that can set you free from bondage now. It will help you actually experience what it means to overcome fear and anxiety through practical strategies that you can employ today. It will help you come to know the confidence and victory that Jesus wants for you regardless of what outside circumstances are affecting your life. And it will increase your absolute certainty in the final outcome of this war, when fear and anxiety and everything else that is evil will be forever destroyed and Jesus wins!

As both a medical doctor and a doctor of ministry I have come to understand how integrated our nature is as human beings. What affects one part of you affects every other part of you, and you can't overcome a problem in one area without involving every other area at the same time. A medical illness will make you more vulnerable to negative thoughts, including fear and anxiety, and it will also make you more vulnerable to Satan's direct attacks against your mind. Conversely a healthy lifestyle will make it easier to take control of your thoughts and increase your sensitivity to what may be happening in the spirit realm. Healthy thinking will both improve your physical well-being and make it easier to recognize attacks from the enemy. Consistent healthy spiritual practices will make all of you—body, soul, and spirit— more resilient to any challenges that may come along. It's not one or another; it's all of the above.

I encourage you to not skip over a chapter as you read simply because you think it doesn't apply to you. Treating a physical problem (for example, diabetes) with a spiritual weapon (for example, pleading the blood of Jesus) is not enough; you will also need to change your eating patterns and perhaps take medication. Likewise, treating a spiritual problem (for example, an attack by Satan against your mind) with physical means (for example, exercise or medication) is not enough; you will also need to learn how to take control of your thoughts and walk in Christ's victory.

It's almost certain that you can—and probably will need to— make changes in multiple areas of your life in order to experience the freedom Jesus has for you and overcome the fear and anxiety that have been holding you in bondage. Don't neglect any area of your life.

Vice Admiral Stockdale maintained faith in his hoped-for

eventual outcome—that the US military would eventually prevail and he and his fellow POWs would be released. When that would happen and whether any one of them would personally live to experience that were uncertain. Regardless of our present circumstances we too can have absolute faith in the eventual outcome of the war in which we fight. That outcome comes in two phases. We know that Jesus has already been victorious over Satan and his kingdom of darkness and that we can live in victory here and now. The victory we can experience is real even though we may still get wounded in the cross fire of a war that continues.

However, this war will not go on forever. We can know with much more certainty than Vice Admiral Stockdale ever had what the final outcome of this conflict will be. Death, sin, Satan, and everything evil will be forever destroyed. We know the end of the story.

And the end of the story is this: Jesus wins!

At the end of each chapter in this book are some questions. If you're reading this book alone, take some time to think about your answers, and perhaps write them down. You are likely to get even more from this book if you read it with a few friends and discuss these questions together.

I'm excited that you are eager to overcome the fear and anxiety in your life, and I'm looking forward to what God will do for, with, and through you as a result. So let's get started.

PART I

THE PROBLEM OF FEAR AND ANXIETY

May the very God of peace sanctify you completely. And I pray to God that your whole spirit, soul, and body be preserved blameless unto the coming of our Lord Jesus Christ.
—1 Thessalonians 5:23

For God has not given us a spirit of fear, but of power and of love and of a sound mind.
—2 Timothy 1:7, nkjv

CHAPTER 1

WHAT'S WRONG WITH ME?

D ENISE WAS A mess. The harder she tried to make things better, the worse they seemed to become. She was exhausted, but whenever she tried to sleep, her mind would switch into overdrive. She would wake up multiple times during the night. Forcing herself to concentrate while meeting with her employees or talking on the phone took more and more of her energy. She felt as if a Boy Scout were practicing his knot tying in her stomach, and there were times when her chest seemed about to explode. When I met her sitting in my office, she struggled to hold back the tears.

Denise had been a Christian for many years, and she worked as an administrator at a Christian school. She was doing what she believed to be God's work but then wondered, "Why am I having such a hard time?" She continually worried about what everyone else thought of her and whether or not she had an illness that would leave her husband a widower. Why couldn't she get a decent night's sleep? She felt guilty for what felt to her like a lack of faith. "Surely God has the answer," she thought.

So Denise revved up her prayer life. She signed up for yet another e-mail devotional that she could read on her tablet during her breaks at work. She asked her husband and two of her friends from church to pray for her. She surveyed her life for anything that might have allowed the devil to enter and create trouble. She tried all the spiritual tactics she had ever heard about.

But still her mind and her heart were constantly racing. She knew she was irritable with everyone around her, but she couldn't seem to change her overreaction to the smallest of inconveniences. And her feelings of fear, failure, isolation, and shame only grew worse as the days went by.

Denise isn't the only Christian who struggles with such a boatload of symptoms. The Bible says, "Be anxious for nothing" (Phil. 4:6). "Do not fear, for I am with you" (Isa. 43:5). But how do you keep yourself from fear? If you're one of the many believers who have tried to fight against fear and anxiety, you know that simply choosing to not be afraid or anxious doesn't work. Those thoughts and feelings seem to take over your body, mind, emotions, relationships with those around you, and spiritual vitality.

You need a plan, a road map, a way through the quagmire of fear and anxiety toward relief. Simply trying harder does not work; if you are reading this book, I'm sure you have already done that. You need someone to help you sort out what is going on and see the steps you can take to get to the other side.

Fear and anxiety can be two of the most distressing problems anyone can experience. You may feel as if some or all of your life is completely out of control.

But it doesn't have to stay that way.

Be assured that you can overcome fear and anxiety! You don't have to just put a bandage on the symptoms and muddle through each day, holding on by your fingernails. You don't have to live paralyzed by fear of both things you can see and things you cannot see. You can understand much about what is going on with you and take the necessary steps to live the fully alive kind of life that Jesus came to bring you in every area (John 10:10). Your journey to relief from anxiety and fear will involve every part of you—and that's a good thing. You can come through this journey stronger and more resilient than ever.

And best of all, through taking this journey you may well learn things about God and about yourself that will make your life so much better than it ever was before. You really can experience His healing, delivering, restoring grace in every part of your being.

I've been where you are. As a young adult I spent several years dealing with multiple symptoms of fear and anxiety. The professionals I saw labeled me with various diagnoses, but things only got worse, and I became almost unable to function during what I euphemistically call "my four years of hell." That is in my past now. Those symptoms are completely gone, and they haven't returned in the nearly twenty years since I found freedom.

I want you to experience that same healing, relief, and joy. I want you to be able to look back and remember the sting but feel it no longer. I want you to have a story to tell to others who may be stuck where you are now.

So will you come along with me?

WHAT IS ANXIETY?

Anxiety is a feeling of apprehension and fear characterized by physical symptoms and feelings of stress. That's a clinical definition of anxiety, the kind of thing a doctor or a psychologist would say.

Anxiety: a feeling of apprehension and fear characterized by physical symptoms and feelings of stress.

But how do you know if anxiety is what you are experiencing? What does it look like? What does it feel like? Each person experiences anxiety and fear in her own way, but here are some of the ways anxiety shows itself:

The mental side of anxiety

The mental and emotional symptoms are the ones most people think of first when you say the word *anxiety*. It can feel as though the accelerator in your mind is stuck in the *on* position, and you can't get the engine to turn off. You can't stop thinking about everything that is going wrong. Even if things aren't especially bad at that moment, you can't stop being afraid of what could go wrong in the future. The rational part of your mind may tell you that you are only worrying about things that will never happen, but your thoughts still do not line up with what your intellect is trying to tell you.

Sometimes your thoughts are not clear at all, and the feelings you experience may be even stronger than your thoughts. You may feel afraid of things that are happening right now and of things that haven't happened yet, or you may not be able to tell what you're afraid of. The feeling persists even if your rational mind tries to tell you that your fear doesn't make sense. You may interpret everything negative around you as evidence that what you're afraid of is just about to happen. You may be unable to notice reassuring signs that your fear is not consistent with reality, and even if you do notice those signs, you remain as upset and tense as ever.

You may feel constantly on edge, tense, and unable to relax. The slightest annoyance may irritate you more than it would someone else. Certain sights, sounds, or smells, or a physical touch may easily startle you. You may feel as though you are waiting for something terrible to happen, and you may or may not know what that is. You may worry that your mind is playing tricks on you and that you cannot completely trust your own perceptions of reality.

Your thinking itself may be affected by anxiety. You may have difficulty concentrating on important tasks in front of you or forget relatively simple things you would normally remember. You may have difficulty forming clear thoughts or making decisions, or you may make hasty decisions that you soon regret.

This picture of fear and anxiety sounds very negative, and if you are the one struggling with such anxiety, it often feels overwhelming. However, many people struggle with a lower level of anxiety. You don't have to experience all these symptoms to be experiencing fear and anxiety. It doesn't matter whether your symptoms are lesser or greater; if your anxious thoughts and feelings are disrupting your ability to live normally and enjoy life, then you are experiencing anxiety.

The physical side of anxiety

The "physical symptoms" referred to in the definition of *anxiety* stated earlier in this chapter are extremely common among those who suffer from anxiety. Some would say that if you have no physical symptoms at all, you may not have significant anxiety. Any part of your body may be affected. Trouble falling asleep or staying asleep is common with anxiety. So are headaches, muscle aches and pains, and a feeling of being tense everywhere in your body. Nausea, diarrhea, abdominal pain, excessive sweating, light-headedness, fatigue and tiredness, heart palpitations, having to use the bathroom urgently and frequently—these are just some of the possible physical symptoms.

Each one of us has, I believe, a physical area where we are most vulnerable. When the ability of your body and mind to cope with whatever is going on becomes overwhelmed, that area of your body can break down. For me that was my GI system; for years it told me exactly when I was feeling anxious or upset. Abdominal pain and cramps, and worse, were the fallout my body took from my fear and anxiety. Many times I had to quickly get off the road and find a bathroom. That hasn't bothered me in many years, so let that be another encouragement that you too can get past your anxiety and its physical symptoms.

The physical symptoms are not all in your head. Your heart really is beating too fast. Your head really does hurt. You really do have to go to the bathroom. God created our bodies to respond to stress in useful and important ways. It is when those stress-induced symptoms are frequent and life altering that they become abnormal. You can think of it as the fight-or-flight response if you wish, and it's built in. Your physical symptoms may be mild or severe, constant or intermittent. If your symptoms are enough to disrupt your life, they are bad enough to take seriously.

It's best to think of these physical symptoms as a sign that something is not OK. It's your body's way of telling you to pay attention; it's a wake-up call, so to speak. Addressing the physical symptoms may sometimes be helpful in itself, but you'll only find true relief when you deal with the fear and anxiety underlying those symptoms.

These physical symptoms bring many patients to see their doctors, and both doctor and patient may not realize at first that anxiety is the underlying cause. In one study 19 percent of patients seeing a primary-care physician had enough anxiety to qualify for an anxiety disorder as the real problem.[1] That's about one in five. Remember, these are very real symptoms; you're not making them up. But there's nothing wrong with your heart or your stomach; the real cause is the fear and anxiety with which your system is struggling.

Up to one in five patients seeking help from a primary-care physician may have physical symptoms caused by anxiety.

We will talk more about dealing with the physical aspects of anxiety in the next chapter. It is not wrong to see your doctor when these symptoms arise; in fact, it's a good idea. Just be open to the possibility that the root of your symptoms may not necessarily be a physical illness.

ANXIETY DISORDERS

We as human beings love putting labels on things. Sometimes that's useful, but it can also lead to pigeonholing someone (you!) into a specific category when it may not completely fit. That's the danger of being labeled with a diagnosis. You're not a statistic; you're a unique human being. Remember that as we talk briefly about the various anxiety disorders as medical diagnoses. If you don't see yourself in exactly one category, that's OK. This book still applies to you.

When anxiety increases to the point that it interferes with one's ability to function adequately in normal daily activities, that person meets criteria for an anxiety disorder. Psychiatrists have put labels on these disorders: generalized anxiety disorder

(GAD), post-traumatic stress disorder (PTSD), obsessive-compulsive disorder (OCD), panic disorder with and without agoraphobia, acute stress disorder, and various phobias. Various physical symptoms are almost always present when anxiety is great enough to qualify as one of these diagnoses. Mental health professionals usually treat such disorders with various medications and/or cognitive behavioral therapy. A large US survey in the early 2000s estimated that during any given year 18 percent of adults—nearly one in five—suffer from an anxiety disorder.[2]

These diagnoses especially apply when your anxiety is out of proportion to what might be considered an average response for a person in similar circumstances and when it persists over a significant period of time. Some circumstances in life are so difficult that nearly anyone would experience anxiety, and we will talk about that specifically in chapter 3. More frequently a level of ongoing fear and anxiety is present that may have no relation to any serious life event. Even more common is a lower level of anxiety that troubles many who may never be diagnosed with an anxiety disorder. This book is not just for those with a diagnosed mental health disorder. It's for you too if you struggle in any way with being afraid and anxious and want to be free from the distress that brings.

Mental health professionals typically differentiate anxiety into two broad categories: trait anxiety, where your personality is characterized by an ongoing anxious approach to the world in general and it adversely affects your life in numerous areas, and state anxiety, where your anxiety is related to a specific and usually temporary stressful circumstance. The questions, suggestions, and spiritual practices talked about in this book apply equally well whether your anxiety is temporary and overwhelming or ongoing and constantly distressing.

There is a lot of overlap in fear and anxiety, and most people struggling with one have symptoms of the other. You may have noticed that fear is included in the clinical definition of *anxiety*. *Fear* can be defined as a thought or a feeling, and *anxiety* as the mental state related to that fear. It is not useful here to worry about the difference. If you are relating to anything you've read so far, this book and the strategies discussed apply to you.

AN INTEGRATED VIEW OF HUMANKIND

You probably already understand that your mind may affect your body, and perhaps you've learned to deal with it to some degree. But you're reading this book because you don't only want to deal with it; you want to overcome fear and anxiety. You want it in your past. I want the same for you too.

How we view our human nature affects how we respond when we face problems. It's true that fighting a spiritual problem with a physical weapon is not likely to get you very far. Likewise, fighting a physical problem with a spiritual weapon may not resolve things as you wish.

Along your journey to finding freedom, it will be helpful to appreciate something of the intricate and integrated way in which God made you. In some Christian circles people describe human beings as "a spirit, having a soul, living in a body." I will never forget the moment when I was born again. (I hope you never forget that moment for yourself as well!) I knew so clearly that some part of me that had not been alive for the first thirty-six years of my life was now alive. God had in some way preserved that core part of my being until that moment, and then my spirit was made alive by His grace.

There is something we miss, however, by focusing on human beings as spirit, soul, and body. These different aspects of our being are not completely separate and distinct entities. When God created Adam, the Bible says he "*became* a living being" (Gen. 2:7). God's breath quickened the coming together of the totality of who Adam was. You are not simply three separate stones sitting on top of one another, or three boxes, fitting inside one another. Instead, you are more like a loaf of bread. You cannot separate the various baked-together parts of you from one another any more than you can separate the flour, eggs, sugar, and salt from that loaf of bread.

Anxiety is the response of your entire integrated human
system to stress that is beyond your usual ability to cope.

Appreciating that interconnectedness is important. It means
that both the cause of and the solution to fear and anxiety—
or any other significant problem—usually involve not just one
aspect. The best way to think about anxiety is that it is the way
you respond whenever the stress you encounter is beyond your
entire human system's ability to cope in its usual ways.

Whatever impacts one aspect of you affects every other part of
you as well. Trying to differentiate the root cause of any problem
has some merit, but most of our problems are not that simple.
You will see later in this book how important it is to cooperate
with God in working through any problem you may have. That
means taking every action that you can in every area of your
life. That may involve making changes in your lifestyle, learning
new thinking patterns, getting expert help when necessary, and
addressing the spiritual aspects of whatever may be going on.

Remember those multiple-choice questions in school? When
dealing with your psychological distress, most of the time the
answer is "d. all of the above."

HOW FEAR AND ANXIETY AFFECT YOUR LIFE

Yes, the emotional and physical symptoms you have are difficult.
You've been living with them every day. But there are probably
many other ways in which anxiety is affecting you, especially if
it is quite severe.

Some forms of anxiety affect people's ability to work and earn
a living, and even if you are able to work, your productivity and
likelihood of promotion may be affected. The worst forms of anxiety may leave you unable to do activities others consider normal,
such as driving or riding in a car, taking a walk, eating in a res-
taurant, or shopping for food. Much of your day may be spent
trying to find ways to work around those limitations, leaving you

with little energy to do anything other than deal with your distress and its ramifications.

You may spend significant amounts of money dealing with and treating your fear and anxiety on visits to mental health professionals and doctors, prescription medication, and other treatments. While progress has been made in health insurance coverage of such disorders, many still must pay for treatment out of their own funds. In 2007 it was estimated that the yearly cost of treating anxiety and related disorders in the United States was $36.8 billion.[3] And the costs keep going up.

The relationship cost of fear and anxiety is also high. You may desperately want to get close to other people but feel unable to do so. Some people don't understand you or how hard you are trying to manage, and they may say or do things that seem hurtful, such as, "You just need to learn not to worry so much." Or, "Don't you believe in God? Just trust Him to take care of things." You may feel isolated and alone even when you're with other people you care about.

Recognizing the many ways in which fear and anxiety affect your life may seem discouraging, but let it motivate you to keep moving forward along the journey to finding relief and freedom.

THE SPIRITUAL COST OF FEAR AND ANXIETY

How your spiritual life is affected by these issues may be somewhat complicated. Perhaps you're similar to Denise, the lady discussed at the beginning of this chapter. As a believer you know God has an answer to your problems, so when you feel anxious or afraid, you go to Him for a solution. There may be times when you feel as though He is helping you. Your prayers seem to calm your mind and perhaps help you rest better.

Other times you feel worse when you pray. You start grasping at anything you can think of to try and get relief from God for your symptoms. You may increase your Bible reading or church attendance, or find various other ways of practicing spiritual warfare. You try to get help from other believers or at a special

Christian event. It may feel like a vicious cycle; the more you struggle to find God's answer, the more anxious you become.

If you are part of a community of faith that teaches and believes that the miracle-working power of God is available for us today, you may struggle with this even more. The harder you pray for a miracle, the more anxious and disappointed you feel when it seems God is doing nothing for you. Others are getting their miracle, so why aren't you? Or perhaps you sense times when God's presence is close to you and you're sure you have found relief. This time your fear and anxiety are gone! But then you become even more frustrated when hours, days, or weeks later it all rushes back to overwhelm you with more force than ever.

Let me assure you that I believe in miracles. I've experienced them. I've seen them. I've prayed for people and seen God do something miraculous in answer to my prayers. I continue to pray for others and for my own needs, and I will do so as long as I'm on this earth. I know without any doubt that God is good, loving, and powerful—and present with us right now.

I have also seen the frustration and disappointment in others and felt it myself when God's answer does not immediately result in complete relief. Any short answer to that frustration would be too superficial, so we'll talk more about it later, and I believe you will find encouragement and hope as you continue to walk this journey to the healing God has for you.

When you struggle with fear and anxiety, you may also find it difficult to relate to God at all. If you've prayed for healing and you haven't experienced it to this point, you may wonder if this Christian thing is really just fake. You may ask, "What's the point of believing God or praying if it doesn't make any difference?" Let me assure you that God hears your cries, and it's OK to ask those kinds of questions. He won't get mad at you. He'll be with you wherever you are.

You may also feel as though you're a royal failure as a Christian if you can't get this under control. After all, the Bible says, "Be anxious for nothing" (Phil. 4:6). So you must be a real screwup if you can't follow those biblical directions. You say to yourself, "No wonder everything's wrong in my life. I'm not doing what God told me to do in His Word. I just have to do better."

And so you try harder and harder, and you become more and more fearful and anxious.

There has to be a better way, and there is. That's why you're reading this book. We've already hinted at part of that answer, and it relates to the integrated way in which God made you. Finding relief from something such as fear and anxiety usually involves all the areas of your life, and we'll look at each of those areas individually. We'll talk about how cooperating with God in all those areas is part of what He desires for you in your journey toward health and well-being.

We'll also talk in detail about what it means to deal with fear and anxiety spiritually. We'll talk about indications that your symptoms may stem from a spiritual problem, and I'll show you a number of specific ways you can practice your faith that will help you find relief. I'll share with you things I learned on my own journey to the other side of fear and anxiety, and I know you'll be glad you didn't give up.

IS ANXIETY ALWAYS NEGATIVE?

Anxiety may almost always feel unpleasant, but it may not always be completely negative. Remember that anxiety generally results when your ability to cope with something stressful becomes overwhelmed. Stress and anxiety are usually closely related. Sometimes you can do something about that stress, and the anxiety may provide a wake-up call so you can make necessary changes.

Can you think of a time when you did something really difficult that ended up bringing positive results? Or a time when you struggled to learn something, such as a difficult subject in school, that's now relatively easy? Perhaps you were able to say good-bye to a destructive relationship or reach a significant achievement in your career. You almost certainly had to overcome some significant anxiety in order to get there.

A measure of anxiety can alert you to the reality that something is wrong and provide the internal energy to take the necessary steps to change, even if those steps prove difficult. Among a group of people who experienced significant and lasting change as a result of some form of therapy, fully 75 percent of those interviewed said a willingness to experience some anxiety along the way was a critically important part of their success.[4]

It is important that you know your goal cannot be the complete absence of all stress and all feelings of tension. Anxiety can be part of God's way of spurring us on to grow and change.

So what does it mean if your physical, emotional, and spiritual symptoms of fear and anxiety are overwhelming? Choose to see your symptoms as a wake-up call. You may not be able to see anything positive at all in your situation, but your anxiety means you're alive and that your body and your mind can respond to what's around you. It means you have some internal energy that can be used to grow and learn and change. It means God can help you take that energy, learn what it's telling you, and focus that energy on becoming who He created you to be.

I'm not making light of your symptoms. Far from it! I know you're miserable and need some relief—as fast as possible. But I also want you to feel real hope. You will find hope here. You'll find understanding and practical steps you can take to help bring relief. And you'll find ways of relating to our wonderful God who wants you to live fully alive in every way.

By the way, Denise found that relief. She made some changes in her lifestyle, and she learned some new thought patterns that made a difference. Treating a medical condition we discovered helped Denise sleep better, and her connection with God grew stronger as she learned some new things about Him as well.

HOPE IN THE MIDST OF FEAR AND ANXIETY

Fear and anxiety are among the most common and distressing mental health conditions affecting people today. The mental and emotional aspects result in a wide variety of physical symptoms that may lead to expensive and frustrating medical care.

God created each human being as a beautiful and integrated whole. What affects one aspect of you also affects every other aspect. A significant problem, such as fear and anxiety, is rarely caused by only one factor, but by a number of factors working together. Likewise, the solution almost always involves looking at the physical, emotional, lifestyle, and spiritual components of who you are as an individual.

Fear and anxiety can have significant spiritual consequences as well as emotional and physical ones. Whatever state you're in right now, you can experience real spiritual growth through cooperating with God in every area of your life.

QUESTIONS FOR CONTEMPLATION AND DISCUSSION

1. Which symptoms of fear and anxiety are most distressing to you? The physical ones? Emotional ones? Spiritual ones?

2. Can you see an example in your own experience of how something that affects one part of you also affects the other areas of your life?

3. Have you been able to see anything good about your anxiety that has helped you feel the internal fuel you needed to accomplish something positive?

CHAPTER 2

PHYSICAL CAUSES OF
FEAR AND ANXIETY

Y OUR HEART IS racing, your stomach is tied in knots, you
hurt all over, and you can't sleep. Is your mind playing
tricks on your body again, or is there really something
physically wrong?

We've talked about the physical symptoms that may be associated with fear and anxiety. There are plenty of circumstances, however, when the arrow points in the other direction and your body is "playing tricks" on your mind. Frequently it's not one or the other, but a combination of both. Your mind and your body can feed off each other. The symptoms of a physical condition or illness may be distressing enough that you feel anxious, which can then make your psychological distress that much worse. And the vicious cycle continues.

As a doctor specializing in women's health I've seen many patients who struggle with nonspecific symptoms that could indicate any number of problems. It's not always possible to completely separate cause and effect or the physical problems from the mental/emotional problems. What's most important is carefully looking at everything that may be contributing to the situation and doing all you can to address whatever is within your control. Sometimes anxiety is the first sign of a significant health issue, and you don't want to ignore that message. Regardless, addressing any physical component of your symptoms is a great place to begin your journey to freedom.

In this chapter we'll look at some things we know about how fear and anxiety relate to physical symptoms, some physical illnesses or conditions that may cause anxiety, and some things you should consider in addressing these physical conditions.

THE STRESS RESPONSE

Your natural stress response is activated whenever you're faced with circumstances beyond your usual ability to manage them. Hans Selye, often considered the father of scientific research on stress, formed much of his understanding of stress based on how he observed people respond to physical stress, such as a life-threatening injury or serious illness.[1] Regardless of whether something is physically wrong or whether the stress begins in your mind, there are certain ways your entire system responds to try to adjust.

It's easy to see how your five senses—sight, hearing, feel/touch, smell, taste—create input that your brain receives and responds to. But all your other internal organs send input to your brain as well. Your nervous system and circulatory system transmit such information throughout your whole body from whatever source it arises. Sometimes your brain responds to those signals by becoming afraid and anxious.

The communication between your gastrointestinal (GI) system and your brain is one of the best examples. Nerve endings in your stomach and intestines are sensitive to the nature of whatever is inside them, such as food, chemicals, liquid, gas, etc. Also, many of the cells lining your stomach and intestines secrete a wide variety of hormones that are picked up by the bloodstream. The variety and quantity of those hormones are affected in part by what you eat. Those nervous and hormonal signals are carried to your brain, which then responds by sending its own nervous and hormonal signals back to your GI system and every other part of your body.

Your brain and your body communicate
constantly through nervous and hormonal
signals. What affects one affects the other.

It's no surprise that certain types of food tend to make you feel sleepy, irritable, or comfortable. (We'll talk a lot more about the important connection between food and anxiety in chapter 5.) There are connections between your brain and most other body systems as well, and when part of your body isn't working well or is ill, your brain usually gets the message. Through these pathways your brain usually knows what's going on in your body even if you're not consciously aware of it. Your emotional state—such as anxiety—may be the way your brain responds to any number of medical or physical issues your body is trying to deal with.

Psychological distress may be your body's way of telling you that something is wrong and asking you to pay attention. It's certainly possible to feel very anxious and have lots of physical symptoms but have nothing physically wrong with your body; that's what the next several chapters are about. But when there is a physical problem, you don't want to ignore the message your brain may be trying to tell you.

GENETIC PREDISPOSITION TO ANXIETY

The genes you were born with affect the ease with which you become afraid or anxious when problems arise and how much of your life you spend dealing with these symptoms. Each of us has a genetic predisposition to handling stress in a certain way, and anxiety may be part of that for you.

If other people in your family have struggled with significant anxiety, it's more likely you will struggle in similar ways. For some years scientists have been looking for specific genes that predispose a person to these problems. It's clear that no one specific gene is responsible; it's usually the complex interaction between your genes, the experiences you had growing up, and other factors in your environment. When a child struggles with anxiety by age eight, it's more likely anxiety will become an ongoing problem in years to come.[2]

Even if you carry a predisposition to anxiety or have struggled with being afraid since childhood, you can still overcome your fears and worries. Each one of us comes into life with stuff to deal with, and this psychological predisposition may be one of those things for you. You may have to work harder at overcoming fear and anxiety than someone else might, but you can still do so. It will be especially important for you to put into practice all the steps talked about in this book in dealing with your symptoms. Remember that God is on your side. He will help you with the wisdom and courage you need to continue to overcome, regardless of your genetic background or the environment around you.

If you have a genetic predisposition to fear and anxiety, you may have to work harder than others at overcoming them, but you can still do so.

MEDICAL PROBLEMS THAT MAY CAUSE FEAR AND ANXIETY

Almost any physical illness or problem may cause your brain to respond with fear and anxiety, and that activity in your brain may in turn increase your physical symptoms. You may already know this if you have been diagnosed with a physical illness. Any illness can be made better or worse depending on the actions you take, and making every effort to manage your illness well will also improve your psychological symptoms.

One frequent cause of fear and anxiety is feeling out of control, and having an illness can certainly make you feel that way. You may be tempted to feel as though your illness has you. Instead of buying into that idea, make the conscious decision to take charge of your illness. Take the time to learn all you can about it—what symptoms to watch out for, what lifestyle changes you may need to make, how to follow appropriate medical advice, etc. Simply gathering enough information and making thoughtful choices about how to deal with your illness may help you feel more in control.

If you don't have a diagnosis of any physical illness, remember that sometimes anxiety is your brain's way of begging for your attention. We'll briefly look at several possible physical causes of fear and anxiety here. This is not an exhaustive list. If one or more of these sounds like it may be a factor for you, discuss it with your doctor.

Cardiovascular (heart) disease

A panic attack and a heart attack may have nearly identical symptoms. The only way to determine which is going on for you may be medical tests at the time you're having symptoms. Some research indicates that ongoing anxiety may also contribute to and predict future heart disease.[3] One of the most frequent things heart disease and anxiety have in common is a fast or abnormal heart rhythm.

That brings up the question of which came first: Did your heart begin beating too fast and cause the anxiety, or did feeling afraid and anxious cause your heart to beat too fast? Wearing a heart monitor for one or several days may provide important information and help your doctor better understand which problem came first. Sometimes it's impossible to definitively answer which came first, and treatment may be focused primarily on improving your symptoms.

Fear and anxiety are also common among people who have had a heart attack or other heart-related health problems. You may have a feeling of doom and have thoughts such as, "Will my heart suddenly stop working?" or "If I do this activity, will it cause my heart too much stress?" If you worry about such things, talking with your heart doctor as well as a mental health professional may be very helpful.

Chronic obstructive pulmonary disease (COPD) and other respiratory problems

When you feel as though you can't breathe, feeling afraid and anxious is understandable. Asthma, chronic obstructive pulmonary disease (COPD), or other respiratory problems may leave you feeling breathless. And when anxiety kicks in, your airways tighten even more, making it difficult to move air in and out. Anxiety and breathlessness become a vicious cycle, each making the other worse. I know how difficult this can be; I watched my husband struggle with anxiety in combination with COPD for a long time.

If you feel short of breath, respiratory function tests can help determine whether you have asthma, COPD, or a related condition. If you do have a respiratory illness, medications or other treatments can greatly improve your quality of life. You can find ways to decrease the environmental triggers that lead you to feel short of breath, and that will decrease your psychological distress also.

Diabetes

Your brain needs a steady supply of glucose—blood sugar—to function normally. If that level becomes too low, your brain cells can become sluggish or stop working entirely. Your body responds to low blood sugar by producing adrenaline, which among other things makes you feel anxious. On the other hand, if your blood sugar becomes too high, your brain cells must divert some of their energy to protecting themselves from too much glucose, and their normal function may also suffer as a result.

If you take medication for diabetes, you know how anxious you can become when your blood sugar falls too low. Eating something that can quickly bring your blood sugar back to normal often solves the problem temporarily.

Nearly 10 percent of Americans have diabetes, but another approximately 25 percent have prediabetes and many of them don't know it.[4] The typical unhealthy American diet, being overweight or obese, and lack of physical activity certainly contribute to this problem. People with prediabetes may have wider blood sugar swings than others, and the lows may contribute to feeling anxious.

The same principle holds when you get really hungry; your brain needs fuel. Eating regular meals of high-quality food and exercising regularly will help your blood sugar remain at more normal levels. (See chapter 5 for more information.) And if that's not enough, medication to treat diabetes or prediabetes may be helpful.

Hormone changes

The dramatic changes in hormones shortly before a woman's menstrual period or during the menopause transition often bring significant psychological symptoms. Anxiety is one of the most common symptoms for women with PMS. With both PMS and menopause the absolute level of estrogen or other female hormones is not important; it's the rapidly changing levels of those hormones that trigger the symptoms of distress.

If you feel anxious only on the days just prior to your monthly period or if you develop anxiety initially around the time of menopause, there's a good chance hormone changes are triggering the problem. Menopause may also trigger an increase in psychological symptoms if you have previously struggled with fear and anxiety.

Hormone changes also make a woman vulnerable right after the birth of a baby. The levels of many hormones plunge once the placenta is gone, adding to all the other things a new mother has to deal with. While postpartum depression has become relatively well known, fear and anxiety can be at least as large a factor for many new moms.

If you're struggling with PMS, menopause, or postpartum depression along with anxiety, you need extra support from people close to you. The lifestyle factors in chapter 5 are especially important. And when necessary, medication (including hormones) may be lifesaving.

Thyroid or other endocrine disorders

Too much thyroid hormone—hyperthyroidism—frequently causes anxiety and many of the associated physical symptoms such as heart palpitations, sweating, insomnia, and muscle tension. Too little thyroid hormone—hypothyroidism—does not usually cause anxiety. However, any thyroid hormone medication used to treat hypothyroidism may cause symptoms of fear and anxiety if the dose is too high.

Optimizing your lifestyle may help you manage the symptoms of a thyroid problem, but it is not likely to do much to help your thyroid itself function better. Usually simple blood tests can determine whether thyroid problems are causing your symptoms, and for most people with hypothyroidism, an appropriate dose of thyroid hormone replacement is easy to determine. There are other times when determining an appropriate dose can be challenging, and it can take months to get it right. If you have hyperthyroidism, sometimes medication will treat the symptoms well enough. Other times radioactive iodine treatment or surgery becomes necessary.

Gastrointestinal problems

Your brain and your GI system are closely connected, as we discussed earlier. GI symptoms are so common with anxiety that it may be difficult to determine which comes first—the nausea, cramping, pain, or diarrhea, or the fear and anxiety. GI symptoms are especially common among survivors of abuse or violence, though there are many other causes as well.

Many GI conditions may cause symptoms similar to anxiety: gastritis, Crohn's disease, various forms of colitis, pancreatitis, irritable bowel syndrome, and more. Sometimes it takes looking inside your GI system with one of a variety of scopes to rule in or rule out one of these problems. Adjusting your diet and other aspects of your lifestyle is usually an important part of managing any of these problems. So is managing your stress level.

Having a label to put on their GI symptoms helps some people feel more in control of their symptoms, and appropriate medications when needed will improve both your unhappy belly and your psychological distress.

Medication side effects

Some people fall into the trap of looking for a pill to fix any problem they have. Other people don't want to take any medication at all, even when necessary and recommended by a medical professional. Neither extreme is wise or healthy. It is true that some people take far too many medications, but other times medication may help you function better, improve your well-being, prevent further complications of your illness, and even save your life. It's important to be thoughtful about any medication you take. See any medications (or supplements) as a tool to use in your journey to better health, not as a fix by themselves.

Anxiety can be a side effect of a wide variety of medications. If your psychological distress started shortly after you began taking a new medication, you may need to work with your doctor to find an alternative. Sometimes the compound effect of a combination of medications will lead to psychological symptoms. The same goes for nutritional supplements; many people don't appreciate how common side effects are with such supplements. If you are taking any prescriptions, over-the-counter medications, or supplements, I suggest you take a complete list to your doctor. Often a pharmacist will be an even better source of help in sorting out whether your specific combination may be causing your side effects.

Stopping the use of certain medications may also lead to anxiety. If you've taken anything to treat your psychological symptoms—prescription or over-the-counter—withdrawing from that medication may lead to a serious increase in anxiety. This is especially true for the class of medications called benzodiazepines. It's wise to discuss things with your doctor before stopping any medication, but especially anything you take for psychological symptoms.

Any time you consider an over-the-counter medication or supplement, or your doctor recommends a prescription, be sure to ask about side effects. Make sure you know what you are taking the medication for, how to take it appropriately, and what to watch out for. Sometimes you may need to deal with mild side effects if the other benefits are important to your overall health.

Drugs or alcohol

Many people try to deal with their fear and anxiety by using drugs or alcohol as an escape. Others begin using those substances "innocently" enough, but now feel they must keep using them in order to function. Dealing with an addiction may cause significant psychological distress, and we'll talk about that more in chapter 3. It's important to realize that the physical aspects of substance use and abuse can lead to serious psychological symptoms. Some drugs may also lead to anxiety as a direct result of their effect on the brain.

When your brain has become accustomed to alcohol or other drugs, stopping their use even for a short time may sometimes cause severe anxiety. Even so, there are few things that will improve your well-being and your future more than overcoming an addiction to such substances. If you struggle with abusing any substance, please get some expert help from a family physician, mental health professional, or treatment center. The physical impact of drug or alcohol use is real, and getting some expert help will significantly improve your chances of gaining freedom.

Chronic pain syndromes

Headaches, muscle aches, pelvic pain, back pain, generalized pain, or any type of chronic pain can become an illness in itself. Pain does a number on your brain. It can take enormous physical and mental energy to deal with chronic pain, leaving precious little energy available for dealing with any other stress. You may struggle to handle normal activities of daily living, not to mention dealing with family or friends who may not understand, medical tests and treatments recommended, and the pressure of holding things together financially. Many factors related to chronic pain may increase your anxiety level.

One of the most important things people with chronic pain must do to improve their well-being is decide to take responsibility for managing their life as a whole. If you suffer from chronic pain, you will need to work very hard to take charge of every aspect of your lifestyle, your thought processes, and your interactions with the health care system. Most people need help in doing this successfully. Look for a professional who is not simply interested in prescribing you a steady dose of pain medication, but who will work with you to find the best ways to manage your symptoms as a whole with or without medication.

TALKING WITH YOUR DOCTOR ABOUT FEAR AND ANXIETY

Health professionals have a role to play in helping you deal with your symptoms, but it's important that you remain in charge. You need their expertise, but they cannot fix you. Remember that no doctor, no hospital, no health food store, no insurance company, and no government program will care as much about your personal well-being as you do. This is your life, your health, and your future we're talking about.

If you haven't already, decide right now to accept responsibility for taking care of your own life and health. You will remain in charge of your health—and your health care.

What does it mean to take charge?

God gave you executive authority over a certain portion of your world. He gave you the ability to make choices, and you're responsible for the outcomes of those choices. That doesn't mean you won't make mistakes; you will. You are not God; He knows what you don't, and He is greater than you in every way. But He has given you the capacity of working together with Him in every area of your life. We'll explore that even more in chapter 6. For now realize that under God you're the one responsible for making decisions based on the best information you have.

It's important that you embrace that personal responsibility as you interact with your doctor and other health care personnel.

They can help, but they cannot fix you. You have more choices than you may realize at every point along the way. One of the most important choices is to see yourself as the manager of your health care—the executive director, so to speak.

When it comes to health care, you may not get everything you want when you want it. The answers to your questions may not be the answers you were hoping for. But you can choose to respond to reality rather than simply react.

You remain in the driver's seat.

Finding the right doctor

Not every medical professional will be interested, willing, or able to help you understand and manage the medical issues that may underlie your fear and anxiety. Recent changes in our US health care system have helped some people obtain health insurance who didn't have it previously, while others have found it more difficult than ever to connect with a doctor. Often you may find yourself interacting with numerous clinics, doctor's offices, or other health care facilities. That may feel frustrating, but remember, you're in charge!

Under God, you're responsible for taking charge of your health—and your health care. You remain in the driver's seat.

Here are a few things to look for when you meet with a doctor for the first time, or to think about when evaluating your relationship with your current doctor:

- Do they listen to me? Health care professionals may have only a few minutes to spend with you— much shorter than they would probably like. Regardless, you should get the sense that you are heard. You should be able to ask any question or bring up any topic and feel reasonably understood.

- Can I work with this doctor as a partner? A good doctor will help you understand your options and respect your decisions. They should talk with you about things you can do yourself to improve your well-being. They should help you learn about your illness, explain things so that you can understand, and be open to at least discussing any treatment options you ask about.

- Do I reasonably like and trust this doctor? Your doctor is not your best friend, but you should feel as though he or she "gets" you, and that they are truly looking out for your best interest.

If your answer to the questions above is no, it may be time to fire your doctor. That's your right, but make sure you are ready to do the hard work of connecting with another doctor.

Tips for talking with your doctor

When visiting your doctor, it pays to do your homework in advance. If you have more than one or two items to discuss, it may be helpful to take a list of questions with you. The clearer you can be about what you want to accomplish at your visit, the more likely you will be satisfied. Being clear is especially important on your first visit. Doctors and the other members of your health care team are people too, and most respond best to clear communication, honesty, and respect.

Often even the best doctor will only give you a moment to explain the reason you came before they begin asking questions or explaining things themselves. That's why it's always best to present your most pressing problem right up front. Briefly explain the problem you think is going on, anything you've tried to do on your own, and your worst fears about the situation. Be ready to answer, "Why did you come in today?"

You might say something such as: "For the past few months I've not been feeling well. I have trouble sleeping, my heart is racing, and I'm tense most of the time. I'm worried that something is wrong with my heart." When you present things in this way your doctor knows what to address, and so do you. You have a shared goal for that visit.

Your doctor will probably ask you a number of follow-up questions. Answer them as clearly and honestly as you can. Don't hold anything back out of fear your doctor may think less of you. Remember your doctor is working for you! Holding back information will only make it less likely that you'll find the real problem. And it's almost certain that your doctor has heard much worse in the past.

Be sure to ask any questions you have as well. No question is a stupid question. Make sure you understand what your doctor thinks may be going on with you. Even if they don't have a diagnosis, they should be able to discuss their ideas of what your problem may be and what they recommend next. If something isn't clear, ask! Before you leave, make sure you understand what you're supposed to do next: Are there any tests you're supposed to take? Any prescriptions to be filled? Any lifestyle changes recommended? When are you supposed to return?

Work together with your doctor to find the best answers and solutions for your symptoms or medical condition. Most doctors find real satisfaction in helping you get better, and by working together you can both reach that goal.

Tests you may consider

What tests you may need depends on the symptoms you are having. This is a short list of some of the tests your doctor may consider. You won't need all these tests, and there may be others you should have depending on your situation. This list assumes you're having significant anxiety that includes physical symptoms and you don't already have a specific medical illness diagnosed.

General laboratory tests

- Chemistry panel: checks basic electrolytes, kidney function, liver function

- CBC (complete blood count): checks for anemia and related problems

- Glucose tolerance test: checks blood sugar over a few hours, used to diagnose diabetes or prediabetes

- Thyroid function tests: may include TSH (thyroid stimulating hormone), T3, T4, and/or others

- FSH (follicle-stimulating hormone): for middle-aged women, may indicate whether she is going through the menopause transition

- Drug levels: if you're taking any medication that needs blood level monitoring

Cardiovascular or respiratory tests (if you have heart or breathing symptoms)

- EKG (electrocardiogram): spot checks heart rhythm

- Holter monitor: measures heart rhythm over a day or several days

- Echocardiogram: ultrasound looking at the function of the heart muscle

- Stress test: using either exercise or a dose of IV medication, checks how your heart responds under stress

- Spirometry: by blowing into a tube, checks you for asthma, COPD, etc.

Gastrointestinal tests (if GI symptoms are present)

- EGD (upper endoscopy): passes a scope down your throat to view your esophagus, stomach, and possibly upper intestines

- Colonoscopy: passes a scope into your colon to check for colitis or other problems

Don't get upset if your doctor doesn't recommend many of these tests. Your situation is unique, and other factors, including your past medical history, will help determine which tests might be most helpful. Don't be afraid to ask questions. And if you have any tests, take responsibility to make sure you know and understand the results.

DEALING WITH YOUR PHYSICAL HEALTH

One important step in overcoming fear and anxiety is doing your best to determine if a medical condition is contributing to your symptoms. Frequently this won't be the only step you need to take, but I urge you to make an appointment with your doctor if you haven't seen one recently. Think through and write down in advance any symptoms you may have, and get checked out.

If you're not certain whether your doctor's recommendations are wise, consider a second opinion. Ask more questions. Pray diligently about it. Part of God's answer for your problem may be helping you and your doctor together find a way to treat your symptoms that improves your well-being both now and in the future. Give Him that chance.

And then keep reading. There are other steps to take in overcoming fear and anxiety and enjoying the fully alive life that God has for you.

NEXT STEPS

Anxiety commonly causes a wide variety of physical symptoms, including sleeplessness, GI symptoms, heart or breathing problems, physical pain, and more. In addition, a number of medical conditions may themselves be the cause of fear and anxiety. Some of the more common ones include heart and lung disorders, abnormal thyroid function, diabetes or prediabetes, hormone changes, and side effects from medications, supplements, or drugs.

If you haven't already, take the time to get a medical evaluation now. Even if you still need to take other steps to overcome fear and anxiety, getting your physical body checked out will put you in a better position to continue your journey to freedom and victory.

QUESTIONS FOR CONTEMPLATION AND DISCUSSION

1. How long has it been since you had a medical checkup? If it's been quite some time, will you make a commitment now to make that appointment?

2. Are there any illnesses you already know you have that may be contributing to your psychological distress? Are you managing your illness(es) the very best way you can?

3. What prescriptions, over-the-counter medications, or supplements are you using? Have you reviewed your complete list with your doctor or pharmacist?

CHAPTER 3

DIFFICULT CIRCUMSTANCES CAUSING FEAR AND ANXIETY

J AMES BEAMED AS he sat down to join us as a guest on our radio program. But he hadn't always felt that positive about life. His father died when James was only twelve. With his mother's support James did well for a few years, but by the time he graduated from high school he was using drugs on the weekends. He dropped out of college a few months later and soon was addicted and living on the streets.

The path to overcoming his addiction was difficult. Treatment involved facing all he had tried to forget about his father's death and learning to be an adult in a world that he had no skills to deal with. He could no longer cover up his worries and fears with a pill or a drink.

Life is difficult—for James, for you, and for me. Bad things happen. Your mind, body, and soul cannot be completely closed to hurtful things that happen around you and to you. To some degree you are vulnerable.

And when you are vulnerable, you are going to get hurt.

Sometimes those wounds are temporary. It's as if your soul gets a cold. It hurts somewhat, but with a little time things heal and you go on with your life.

Other times those wounds are deep: childhood abuse that goes on for years, feeling trapped in a violent or destructive marriage, an addiction establishing its hooks in your brain, a natural disaster or accident that permanently alters your life, or watching an important person in your life die. Your very best mental, physical, and spiritual coping mechanisms aren't enough to get things back to normal. Your world is changed forever.

Your brain responds to these disrupting circumstances in many ways, including with fear and anxiety. You will likely handle difficult circumstances differently from anyone else; that's normal. Some traumas are so disrupting that even the strongest person would suffer serious distress. You may be thinking about disrupting circumstances in your own life. Don't spend time wondering whether the circumstances are bad enough to cause the amount of distress you now feel. The way you are responding is just that; it's your way, and you deserve to be taken seriously.

Let's look at some of the ways you may respond to difficult circumstances and some specific traumas you may have experienced. I have some suggestions on how you can find healing in spite of, and even because of, the difficulties you face.

YOUR BRAIN'S RESPONSE TO TRAUMA

Some of the best research on trauma has looked at people who experienced exceptionally severe life disruptions: former prisoners of war, adults who experienced long-term abuse as children, loved ones of someone who died, or survivors of terrorist attacks. Those are circumstances when any human being's coping mechanisms could be overwhelmed. Such stories help us understand some of what your brain does when faced with difficult circumstances and provide elements that may help you find a good life again on the other side.

Keep in mind that even if your difficult circumstances don't seem as bad, your brain may still respond in similar ways. If you're struggling with psychological distress, it's helpful to survey your past and present for any unfinished business—traumas you haven't completely dealt with or healed from.

Some scientists and mental health professionals have built entire careers around studying trauma or treating individuals so affected. But here are two concepts I believe are especially helpful as you look at how difficult circumstances may be affecting your fear, anxiety, and related symptoms.

First, you will be affected both internally and externally by your difficult circumstances. The external (or visible) effects may be easier to appreciate at first. Your physical health and/or your finances may be impacted. Your former way of living may be impossible to go back to. Other people may have forced you into circumstances that you cannot change.

But the internal effects are frequently as or more impactful than the external ones. Your sense of safety and stability in the world may be shattered, or it was never able to develop at all. Your identity as a person might be altered. Your faith in your own ability to think, make decisions, and have your decisions make a difference may be broken. Your ability to trust God or other people may be shaken.

The internal effects of those difficult circumstances will likely last longer and be more difficult to deal with than the direct circumstances themselves. Trying to ignore those internal effects does not make them go away. The only way to lessen their hold on you is to face them and bring them into the light. If you do not do this fully, they will eat away at your insides. Your body will likely take the brunt of the impact, and your physical symptoms will continue and perhaps worsen until you deal with what happened or is happening. That's why many (not all!) people with a chronic illness also suffer from unhealed trauma from child abuse or unresolved bitterness over past wrongs.

Second, you have a choice about how you respond to even the most difficult and damaging circumstances. This may be difficult to appreciate when you're in the middle of tough stuff. You likely feel you have no control, which only adds to your anxiety and distress. And yet you always have more choices than you realize.

Who would have less control over their circumstances than prisoners of war? But remember Vice Admiral Stockdale? Not all POWs develop post-traumatic stress disorder (PTSD), and some who do are able to overcome their symptoms and go on living well. One research study showed that POWs who chose to mentally focus on something good—such as thinking about the eventual end of the war or family they knew were praying for their return—experienced the best mental health outcomes and positive growth after their harrowing experience.[1]

Choosing how you respond does not mean ignoring or refusing to acknowledge the unfairness, pain, destructiveness, or perhaps very real evil of your reality. (Remember the Stockdale paradox.) Instead it means being completely honest about the things that are outside your control but choosing to spend most of your energy focused on the things that are within your control. And there are always things that are within your control. As the POWs' stories illustrate, even if you can't control anything in your environment, you can always choose what to think about. Most of the time you have other choices as well.

One of the best expressions of this I know is the Serenity Prayer: "God, grant me the serenity to accept the things I cannot change, the courage to change the things I can, and the wisdom to know the difference." May you find the wisdom to know what you can change and the courage to take the actions that you can. I pray this book will be instrumental in helping you find the wisdom to know the difference.

WHAT DOES HEALING LOOK LIKE?

What do you imagine healing looks like? Does it mean you will be exactly the same as you were before the traumatic experience? Will your mind and body be as though they were never hurt? If you're struggling with fear and anxiety right now, that may be the outcome you wish for. You may be searching for a way to make it all go away—some magic pill, new therapy, spiritual warfare technique, or special event or person to make it all OK again. But that's not usually the way human minds and bodies work, and it's not usually the kind of healing God has in store for you. You won't be able to jump over or slide around the edges of trauma—you have to go through. Sometimes that means the fear and anxiety will temporarily get worse before they get better. And it usually means you will need someone to walk that journey with you—a caring and wise friend, a support group, or a knowledgeable therapist.

The healing that you can expect from such a journey will be uniquely yours, and it will be tailored by God just for you. Later in this chapter we'll talk about some aspects of this journey that you may find helpful and some tasks that you can focus on along the way. Even on your hardest days, hold on to hope. Things don't have to remain as difficult as they are now. God has something better for you.

Healing for you will probably mean that you remember what happened, but it won't hold control over your life any longer. The abuse, the addiction, the loss, the trauma will have lost its sting. You will be different than you were before, but not all those differences will be negative. You will discover strengths you didn't realize you had, things about God you never knew before, and gifts in your own heart that you have to give to others that you never knew were there.

Now let's look at some of the common types of difficult circumstances that can lead to such psychological distress. If your trauma is not listed here, don't worry. Remember that whatever your "stuff" is, it's worth taking seriously.

TRAUMAS THAT MAY CAUSE FEAR AND ANXIETY

I've used the word *traumas* here only because I don't know a better word. We only have space here to discuss some of the more frequent or obvious traumas that may cause fear and anxiety. But any circumstance that causes you significant stress or harm is a trauma. Remember, it's not how someone else would grade the seriousness of your experience that's important; it's how that experience has affected you that matters.

Child abuse and bullying

The effects of physical, sexual, emotional, or verbal abuse that happened to you as a child don't go away just because you grow up. That abuse may be especially damaging when it was perpetrated by someone who was supposed to care for you, such as a parent, grandparent, older sibling, stepparent, other relative, teacher, coach, or friend. Associated physical symptoms can include headaches, pelvic pain, GI problems, and more. Panic attacks, PTSD, anxiety, depression, and any variety of psychological distress is also common.

The Los Angeles Unified School District is responsible for more than 650,000 students. Pia Escudero, the director of school mental health, reported than when they screened their students for trauma, 98 percent of them reported at least one traumatic event, and most of them had experienced several. Not all that trauma was abuse; they also screened for things such as homelessness or having a parent incarcerated. But the 98 percent number is truly astounding. While twenty-first-century Los Angeles may be an especially traumatic place for children to grow up, it still speaks to how common these problems are.[2]

Bullying may seem like comparatively innocent child's play to onlookers, but both those who bully and those who are bullied may develop significant psychiatric symptoms in the future. A recent study in the United Kingdom demonstrated that the psychological effects of bullying often persisted for at least forty years and significantly affected adult quality of life.[3]

If you experienced abuse, bullying, or some other trauma during your early years, there is almost certainly a direct relationship between those experiences and your psychological distress now. Simply deciding to not allow it to affect you doesn't work. For you to experience healing, it's important for you to find a safe place to tell your stories. You need caring and honest feedback from people who understand you. You will probably find that a support group and/or therapist who specializes in the effects of childhood trauma is helpful.

Dysfunctional family dynamics

Are there any completely functional families around? I'd like to meet one. Every family has their ways of behaving that they learned from the generations before them. You'll naturally pick up those same ways of behaving unless and until you examine your family heritage openly and honestly, make conscious choices about what to keep and what to leave behind, and work diligently to learn new ways of behaving in those areas you choose to change.

Of course some families are more dysfunctional than others. Some of the family dynamics that are likely to cause ongoing anxiety-related problems include mental illness, violence, addiction, abuse, incarceration, or other forms of instability. These issues may overlap with childhood abuse. You may currently feel manipulated by overly controlling family members, or you may have ended some relationships because they were so disruptive to your life.

In any family there's more than enough blame to go around. They did things to each other. They did things to you. You did things to them. Nobody responded well. And in the current mess nobody knows where the problems began or what to do about them. Such family chaos may continue to affect your psychological well-being whether or not you have a current relationship with the problem family members, and you may have contributed your own share to the chaos.

Moving past such family dynamics involves some serious maturity on your part. The skills talked about in this book—forgiveness, taking responsibility for your own actions, learning to say no, and others—can help you become the person God created you to be regardless of your family background. Simply looking at something in your family history and saying, "I don't want to repeat that," is not enough. It's a start, but you will then need to consciously learn a new way of thinking, speaking, and behaving in that area, whether it be expressing emotions, money management, handling conflict, sexuality, or whatever you want to do differently.

Addiction

Addiction is complicated. Addiction is certainly more than an external circumstance causing you fear and anxiety, but it does deal with external stimulus. Pills, drugs, alcohol, gambling, sex, tobacco—you may have started using that substance or behavior to try and deal with some stressful experience you were having, or perhaps you began for a different reason. But now the psychological distress of the addiction is only one more hook in your brain that seems to give your fear and anxiety control over you.

Finding freedom from an addiction involves addressing all the ways it has affected you—your physical health, your mental thinking, your emotions, your past, your social relationships, and your spiritual well-being. Each area needs to be honestly looked at, brought into the light of God's presence, and allowed to heal.

There has been a lot of discussion among doctors and mental health professionals about whether or not addiction is a disease. Thinking of it as a disease makes sense in many ways. You certainly don't wake up one day and decide to be addicted. There are genetic factors involved, and there are very real biological affects in your body and your mind. However, if thinking of addiction as a disease prevents you from taking complete responsibility for your actions, then it is a dangerous concept. Regardless of the factors involved, you are responsible for taking whatever steps are necessary to get help and live in freedom from your addiction.

That does not mean you can find freedom on your own. You may need a team to help you—doctors, therapists, other addicts who are finding freedom—and more than anything else God's grace. Spiritual warfare, discussed later in this book, is often important, but it is only one tool in the process of breaking free. It may help to think of your addiction as a devastating problem you have, but a problem that is separate from your identity as a person. There's a you in there that other people can help you discover, that Jesus died for, and that God wants to set free. Get some help, and don't give up.

Violence

Domestic or intimate partner violence creates invisible wounds that remain long after any physical injury is healed. It may be safer to talk about this now than it was some years ago, but that does not mean it is easy. It may be easier to say "My heart is racing, and I can't sleep" than to talk about your spouse's fits of rage and the physical injuries you've sustained. It may feel more acceptable to talk about your stomach pains than the verbal beatings or sexual exploitation you get from your boyfriend. Statistically women are more commonly the victims in violent relationships, but men can be victims too.

A random shooting, stranger rape, a terror attack, being in a war zone—these are only some of the violent circumstances that may trigger serious anxiety and all the physical and emotional symptoms that may result.

Extricating yourself from a violent relationship or healing from PTSD after being in a war zone or experiencing a sexual assault is too big a topic to cover completely in this chapter. We talk about violence here in order to acknowledge that it is much too common and that it may very well be the experience that has set up the psychological distress you face now. Lifestyle measures, practicing good thinking, and prayer may all be helpful. But you will only be able to resolve the effects of trauma on your body and mind by dealing with it directly. Thankfully trauma specialists are more available now than ever. Find one, and get some help.

Death and grief

I'm writing this only weeks after the death of my loving husband. I had anticipated the feelings of sadness and loss, but I have been surprised by how much anxiety I have also experienced. My world has been ruptured, and my mind has been struggling to reorient, to think, to make sense of what doesn't make sense.

If you've lost someone close to you—a parent, a spouse, a child, a sibling, a good friend—you may be facing something similar. There's no way to put grief into a neat little package. There are many more elements to grief than anxiety, but it's important to acknowledge that the death of someone close to you is one of the most stressful experiences any human being can go through. That amount of stress is enough in itself to lead you to feel disoriented, anxious, fearful, and traumatized.

If you've struggled with fear and anxiety in other areas of your life, the death of a loved one may very well stir up those same symptoms again, including physical symptoms. That doesn't mean you're weak or have lost any previous victory you experienced. Death is an aberration in the way God created us. He didn't intend us to live some years, even many years, on this earth and then die. He created us to live forever. Death may be normal for this earth, but it's not normal for God's universe. Feeling anxious about something God never originally intended is normal.

Don't allow yourself to get more worried and afraid because you feel upset after a loved one's death. This is a time to be gentle with yourself and to ask for support. Find a friend or a group such as GriefShare where you can express your feelings, and allow them to minister God's comfort to you.[4] What you're feeling is normal, and it can get better if you do the work of mourning.

Effects of trauma

These are only some of the difficult circumstances that may be disrupting and anxiety-producing for you. The way any trauma affects you will depend on many things, including your age at the time it happened, your personality, how much you feel or felt in control in other areas of your life, how much support you had then or have now, and more. If you know that some difficult circumstance has been a trigger for your psychological distress, that's the place to start. Remember, what's important is not how bad the event was or is, but how it has affected you. The tasks we'll discuss next are likely to be helpful in your journey to wholeness regardless of the type of trauma you have experienced or how long it's been.

MOVING PAST TRAUMA TO HEALING

Time alone does not heal. The passing of time may allow a scar to form over the surface of your trauma wound, but if what's underneath is not addressed and allowed to heal, the pain and injury will continue. You'll still be that five-year-old little girl hiding under the bed hoping your alcoholic father won't find you. Or you'll still be looking over your shoulder and startling at any strange sound twenty years after your rape. You'll cringe any time another person touches you a certain way, or white-knuckle it to keep from taking that narcotic pill when you feel upset. You'll refuse to go to your high school reunion because your old bully will be there, or still feel as angry about your loved one's death as you did the first month after she passed away. That's not healing.

The only way time heals is if you actively engage in healing activities during that time. Healing is not passive, and it doesn't just happen to you. Healing is something you actively participate in, search for, work toward, find, and experience. You can't do it alone; you need other people along the way, and you most certainly need God's healing, delivering presence for that healing to happen. Don't wear yourself out, but you must be active in the process.

Here are some ways you can actively participate in your healing. These are important regardless of how long it's been since your difficult experience, or how small or large the trauma was.

Listen to your body and your mind.

Acknowledging that you feel afraid, anxious, or otherwise distressed is a good starting point. It helps you own something about what is going on with you. It's one part of your truth, and without owning it as your own you can't take the next step.

You can also find out more by listening more intensely to your body and mind, and even asking questions of them. Notice what thoughts are going through your mind when you feel upset. (We'll talk more about this in chapter 4.) Notice how your body feels when you have those thoughts. Notice what just happened and any triggers around you that made you feel afraid or anxious.

You may also notice other feelings underneath or in addition to fear and anxiety. Those may include anger, fatigue, confusion, a sense of loss, powerlessness, or others. Become sensitive to the signals in your physical body to begin to understand what you're feeling and perhaps why. You can use the things you come to understand about yourself to find safe people and places to get support and discover other activities that help you find healing.

Feelings are not everything. Learning to listen to your body and mind is only one step to finding healing. You'll also need to take further steps that will, over time, change how you feel. Your feelings give you important information about yourself and your circumstances. Feelings are true, but feelings are not the whole truth.

Learn healthy ways of expressing your feelings.

If you've struggled with fear and anxiety for a long time, feeling fear and anxiety is the primary way you've expressed your feelings. It will be helpful for you to learn other, more useful ways of expressing those same feelings. What that looks like will depend on your personality and choices.

It's hard to overstate the benefit of talking with safe people about your difficult circumstances. Other survivors of child abuse, domestic violence, or wartime or any other trauma can be an invaluable help to you. Such conversations can help you feel validated. You may feel hopeful as you see others who are further along in their journey, and you will feel stronger as you offer support to others who are not as far along as you. Look for a person who will allow you to be real but also help you find positive ways to express your feelings.

Listen to your feelings; they give you
important information. Your feelings are
true, but they are not the whole truth.

Crying, writing, drawing, painting, singing, and yelling (not at someone else) are some ways to express your feelings. All of that is OK—even if you're yelling at God. Remember that He's the only One completely capable of understanding you and who will be with you always. Harming other people or property—or yourself— is never appropriate. If you find yourself struggling with the urge to harm yourself or others, get help right away. If you can't think of anywhere else to get help, in the United States you can call a national help line: 1-800-273-8255 (1-800-273-TALK).

Take one step at a time.

You can't feel and heal from a trauma in one moment. You feel psychological distress after trauma because your normal coping mechanisms were completely overwhelmed. It's important to take the journey forward in small doses. There are no medals given for speed; what's important is that you keep taking steps in the direction of your healing.

Your journey to healing is probably taking longer than you think it should. Don't let worrying about that add more distress to the load you're already carrying. Consider keeping a journal of your journey to wholeness. Write anything you wish, but especially about the things you're learning about your body and mind, the steps you're taking to find healing, and any small successes along the way. When you get discouraged about the process, reading something you wrote weeks or months ago may help you feel encouraged about the progress you've made.

If you wonder where to begin in your healing journey, here are some steps that may help you get started:

- Write down what happened and how it affected you.

- Choose one safe person or group to talk to about your experience.

- Think or write about anything that triggered your fear and anxiety today.

- Think or write about something healthy that helped you feel better—a song, a conversation, a good night's sleep, a prayer, etc.

Make choices where you can.

One major part of psychological distress is the sense of being out of control—both about what happened and about how it's affecting you now. Every small way you can take back that sense of control will be helpful in your journey to healing.

Think of the choices you do have right now. Perhaps you can't imagine living without alcohol, but you can find the nearest Alcoholics Anonymous group and go to a meeting. Perhaps you can't begin to imagine not being controlled by your mother, but you can let her next phone call go to voice mail and respond when you feel ready.

Practicing making choices in unrelated areas will help you, so stretch yourself in small ways. Try new food. Choose something different to wear. Choose to talk to a coworker who seems safe. Simply making a small choice and taking action will stretch you and empower you for the next step.

Coping through religion

You're reading this book because at least a part of you believes God has an answer for your psychological distress. That belief is powerful. Discovering God's answer for your distress involves more than praying "God, please help me!" and then waiting for Him to do something. Your action and cooperation along the way make a great difference.

Being connected to a supportive community of faith has been shown repeatedly to be beneficial for those who have experienced or are experiencing trauma.[5] It's more than simply attending services, although that helps. It's the connection with people that is most helpful. Hopefully you are planted in a church where you find help and support. If not, there's no better time than now to connect with some group in the body of Christ. No church is perfect, but being connected to other growing believers will be beneficial in healing from whatever trauma has impacted your life.

If you have been hurt, you will have to face the matter of forgiveness. You won't find freedom and joy until you deal with this head-on. Forgiveness is not saying that what happened to you is OK. It's not OK! That's why forgiveness is the only way you can find freedom from the trauma's hold on you. Forgiveness is giving up the right to continue to be hurt by the person who hurt you. It's making the choice to let God deal with them since you can't do it anyway. If that person is still destructive, you may have to protect yourself from being hurt further. But you can forgive someone whether or not you choose to continue a relationship with them.

If you struggle with the whole area of forgiveness, you're not alone. Remember that forgiveness is a choice, and it takes time. Give God permission to continue working with you in this area, and He will do so.

BEGIN HEALING

Your brain responds to difficult or traumatic circumstances in understandable and individually unique ways. If some trauma in your past or present has precipitated your psychological distress, dealing with that circumstance is the place to begin. Your journey to healing may be longer than you hoped, but healing is possible.

Child abuse, bullying, dysfunctional family dynamics, violence, addiction, and the death of someone close to you are only some of the traumas that frequently lead to fear and anxiety. Your active participation in the journey will be necessary to find healing. You can do that by taking such steps as learning to listen to your body and mind, finding healthy ways to express feelings, making active choices where you can, and working together with God to find the healing He has for you.

QUESTIONS FOR CONTEMPLATION AND DISCUSSION

1. What are the difficult circumstances in your past or present that are affecting your psychological distress now?

2. How have you been trying to cover over the effects of that trauma instead of working openly to find healing?

3. How has your faith affected your journey toward healing from trauma? How has it been a help? Are there ways in which it has been a hindrance?

CHAPTER 4

THE ROLE OF YOUR MIND

WHAT'S GOING ON in your mind right now? Before reading any farther, take stock of what thoughts and feelings are there.

Any number of things could be going through your mind: "My coworker sure made a mess of things today. It will take me three days to straighten it all out." "I wonder what my son and his friends are doing right now. They're probably up to no good." "I dread going to the doctor this week. I'm sure it will be bad news." "My husband never notices when I'm tired or upset. All he thinks about is himself."

Your mind never truly shuts off. It may be wandering or focused, creative or confused, upbeat or upset. Thoughts and feelings get mixed up together until we find it hard to differentiate one from the other. Emotions are a big part of what goes on in your mind, and you may not be able to change your feelings simply by wanting to. But you *can* change your thoughts, and over time those new thoughts will lead to changed feelings.

This chapter is about the part of your mind that you have conscious control over and about how your choices in that area affect those parts of your mind that you can't control. You can't change the present facts of your coworker's or your son's actions, the doctor's report this week, or your husband's personality, but you have enormous power in deciding how you think about those facts or even whether to think about them at all. In fact, you can control more than you probably realize.

Fear and anxiety involve both thoughts and feelings. Choosing what thoughts you spend time thinking will affect how you feel. This is not the only area of your life you need to take charge of, but if you want to overcome fear and anxiety and experience the fully alive life God wants for you, it is critically important for you to take charge of your thought life.

There is one thing we need to make clear: your thoughts are powerful, but they are not all-powerful. You can change many things about how you feel by changing your thoughts, but you cannot change everything. This is not "mind over matter." It's important to give your thoughts the appropriate amount of credit—not too little or too much. It's more likely that you place too little emphasis on what you think rather than too much. I did for many years, and my life became dramatically better when I learned I could choose my thoughts—and in time that would change my feelings.

THE BIBLE AND YOUR THINKING

God's Word has a lot to say about your thoughts. The Bible assumes that when God asks us to do something with our thoughts, we are capable of following His direction. We may not do it perfectly; we need God's forgiveness, grace, and delivering power to have a free and clear mind. But we can make an effort, and we are capable of making progress.

What should you think about? God told Joshua to "meditate on [this book] day and night," and that doing so would lead him to be successful in the mission God gave him (Josh. 1:8). In the Psalms we're encouraged to meditate on God Himself and on the good things God has done in the past (Ps. 63:6; 77:12). Thinking about God, His word, and what He has done for you are certainly good things to think about, but there are more.

It takes effort to keep your thoughts where they should be. When David was in distress, he didn't wallow in worry but resolutely told himself, "Why are you cast down, O my soul? And why are you disquieted in me? Hope in God" (Ps. 42:5). Peter encouraged believers to "guard your minds" (1 Pet. 1:13). That's a picture of decisively choosing what your mind will do rather than letting your mind think and feel whatever comes most easily.

Paul made the clearest statements of all about what believers should do with their thoughts. You may have heard this verse many times: "Finally, brothers, whatever things are true, whatever things are honest, whatever things are just, whatever things are pure, whatever things are lovely, whatever things are of good report, if there is any virtue, and if there is any praise, think on these things" (Phil. 4:8). That doesn't mean refusing to see problems when they arise or being less than honest about your struggles, but you have a choice about what your mind focuses on, and placing the majority of your mental energy toward these positive things is healthy.

Paul is even more specific in 2 Corinthians, where he writes, "Bringing every thought into captivity to the obedience of Christ" (2 Cor. 10:5). That's a very tall order. If your thoughts aren't serving you—or Christ's purpose in you—well, it's time to get strong or even militant about examining what you think about. Then check every thought against what God has to say. That's the standard the Bible sets for your thinking.

So how do you do all that? You can't think only about God, His Word, and what He has done for you every moment. There are other things you have to deal with—work and family responsibilities, problems, thoughts you can't seem to get control of, or negative stuff that won't go out of your mind.

Let's get extremely practical and look at what it means for you and me in the twenty-first century to take control of our thinking as God's Word says we should. By doing so, you will have some amazing tools to deal with fear, anxiety, and any type of psychological distress. These skills will teach you to take control of your mind, as Paul indicated we must do.

NOTICE YOUR THOUGHT HABITS

Habits make our lives easier. Because of your habits, you don't have to think about how to take a shower, what route to take to work, or what that "ding" coming from your phone means. You develop habits in the way you think, as well. Some of those thought habits serve you well, and others don't. If you struggle with long-standing fear and anxiety, your thought habits probably need a tune-up or perhaps a significant overhaul.

You didn't develop these thought habits overnight. Many factors contributed to their development: childhood experiences, your personality, things other people have said to you, media you've consumed, choices you've made, and more. One of the first steps in getting control of your thinking is to notice the thoughts you are already thinking. If you feel distressed, ask yourself, "What am I thinking right now?" And then ask yourself, "Why am I thinking that?"

Do not beat yourself up if you're not happy about your thoughts, but notice and try to understand what you're thinking. You might tend to focus on a terrible outcome that may or may not happen, or become consumed with what other people are thinking about you. You might be rehearsing negative experiences from your past or telling yourself all the reasons why you're a failure and incapable of succeeding.

When you begin asking yourself why, you may understand better some of the circumstances that led you to develop those thought habits. Remember, your purpose here is to notice and understand first, not to berate yourself. Listen to what your mind is telling you. Think of yourself as an observer watching your brain work.

Ask yourself: "What am I thinking right
now?" and "Why am I thinking that?"

At first you'll probably forget to notice your thoughts for periods of time. When evening comes or the next day, you'll suddenly remember and say to yourself, "What was I thinking?" That's normal. You may find that keeping a journal will help you develop the new habit of noticing your thoughts. I kept a daily journal for many years, and I still make use of it when I'm feeling unsettled. Writing down your thoughts helps you understand them better. You may even feel more in control simply by getting your thoughts written down.

Don't park here. Endless self-analysis isn't the goal. The purpose is to help you objectively identify frequent thoughts you have so that you can "bring them into captivity," as Paul instructed. We'll talk about how to do that as we continue.

YOUR LIFESTYLE AFFECTS YOUR THINKING

How much sleep did you get last night? What did you have to eat for your last meal? Those and many other factors definitely impact not only your feelings but also your thoughts. Remember the Snickers commercials where the announcer says "You're not yourself when you're hungry." Not that candy is an appropriate stress reliever! You can probably think of times when a problem seemed overwhelming in the evening but seemed much more manageable after some hours of sleep.

These are some factors that will affect your thinking:

- What you eat and drink. Your brain needs a regular supply of water, glucose, amino acids, and healthy fats to function well. Drinking plenty of water and eating a balanced diet of mostly unprocessed foods make it easier to choose your thoughts.

- Physical exercise. Your brain needs oxygen, and physical exercise improves oxygen delivery to your whole body, including your brain. The endorphins that increase with exercise also help your brain think more positively.

- Rest. A mind that's tired for any reason—lack of sleep, stress, or mental or emotional overwork—cannot think as clearly. Rest improves both your mood and your ability to control your thinking.

- People around you. Spending time around positive people will help your mind notice positive things and think positive thoughts. Your family, friends, and coworkers affect how your mind functions.

We'll talk more about lifestyle choices in chapter 5, but for now notice how your mind thinks differently depending on these factors. If you're tired and hungry, you may think, "I'll never get this project completed," or "Everyone thinks I'm a failure." After some sleep, a brisk walk, a healthy meal, or a good talk with a friend, you may think, "This is a huge challenge, but I'm going to make steady progress," or "That wasn't a smart decision. I can learn from it and do better next time." See the difference?

Part of learning to take charge of your thinking—"bringing every thought into captivity"—is learning the lifestyle measures that will help you do so. If you're struggling to control your thoughts, consider what improvements you can make in your lifestyle.

GARBAGE IN, GARBAGE OUT

I learned basic computer programming as a senior in high school—using the old eighty-column paper punch cards. If one little hole was punched wrong, the output would be completely meaningless. We were told, "Garbage in, garbage out."

In many ways your mind is similar to a computer. Your neurons, blood vessels, and other anatomy is similar to hardware. Food and oxygen are their power supply. Your brain cannot function without these basics in place. That's why paying attention to your physical health makes such a difference in your mental and emotional well-being. But that's just one step.

The input you allow into your mind is like the input your

computer receives—stuff you download from the Internet, pictures you input from your phone, words you type, etc. The programs on your computer can't do anything unless you give them the appropriate input. So it is with your mind.

Think of the messages—the input—your brain received today. You may have watched the news as you prepared for your day and listened to the radio on your way to work. Your spouse, children, or other family members may have complained, worried, or blamed you for something this morning. Your boss may have come down hard on you, or your coworkers let you know they were unhappy with your performance. Internet ads barraged you when you checked your e-mail, and you certainly noticed the socially acceptable posts from your friends on Facebook. In the pharmacy aisle on your way home you couldn't escape the displays touting the weight-loss or energy-boosting properties of the latest product, and the tabloids at the checkout counter let you know that other people's lives are more interesting than yours. Your mail reminded you of your financial obligations. At home the evening news dramatized how the world is falling apart, and the standard prime time programming capitalized on sex, violence, and sensational reality.

Whew! Did just reading that list make you feel uptight all over again? Can you see how the input you allow into your mind affects your thoughts and how your brain functions?

You're working on learning to notice your thoughts. Learn also to notice the messages that are coming into your mind that may sound like your own thoughts but are more likely to be what the media want you to think. The messages might sound something like this:

- "Your life isn't interesting or meaningful."

- "Your family, your job, your life doesn't measure up."

- "You're a failure if you don't do this or accomplish that."

- "You need to lose weight (or buy this product or join this group) in order to be OK."

- "The government, financial stability, our way of life—it's all about to collapse."

Mindlessly taking in these daily messages is certain to leave you frustrated, sad, afraid, anxious, or upset. For high-quality thoughts and feelings, pay attention to the messages you allow in your mind. You cannot completely ignore all the negative messages, but you don't have to blindly accept what those messages would have you think. You can choose the input you want your mind to receive; choose input that will help you move toward "taking every thought captive." And you can choose what to do with the messages your mind does take in.

CHOOSE THE INPUT YOUR MIND RECEIVES

You can't live in a bubble, but you must put a filter on the gateways to your mind and be intentional about what you let through. If you don't, your mind will passively accept whatever disturbing, stressful, overwhelming, or potentially evil diet your environment decides to serve up. If you actively take charge of your mind's input, your thoughts will have much more positive "fuel" with which to work.

First, consider what negative input you can decrease or eliminate. That input usually comes from either negative people or the broad category we call media. Here's a news flash: you don't have to give everyone the same access to your life just because they expect it! Some people can make you feel angry or sad or upset just by being in their presence. Your good day suddenly turns dark when they come around. You can take control. If that person doesn't have anything to give you and if he isn't able to accept anything you have to give him, decrease the amount of time you spend around him. And don't be too quick to say you can't. If that person is your parent, limit the frequency of your calls or visits and have someone else with you when you are there. If that person is your boss, you can still choose to limit your contact or even consider changing jobs.

---

*If you want high-quality thoughts and
feelings, pay attention to the type of media
and messages you allow into your mind.*

But what if that difficult person is closer to home, such as your spouse or child? Hearing constant negative input from someone so close to you is discouraging. If your spouse is a person of good will, they may respond to a conversation about what kind of help you need to be more positive. If it's your child, you can talk with other parents with similar struggles to help you maintain perspective. If your spouse is regularly destructive and not willing to work on your relationship, it's time to get some help.

The other broad category of input is media: Internet sites, TV programs, music, books, magazines, podcasts, videos, social media, etc. It's so easy to consume what's popular or entertaining without paying adequate attention to its effect on your mind. Run the media you consume through Paul's filter in Philippians 4:8. I don't believe Christians need to limit their media consumption to overtly Christian sources, but whatever you allow into your mind will have an effect. You may need to make some tough choices to stop taking in some of the material you're accustomed to.

Quantity matters as well as quality. If you struggle with fear and anxiety, constantly watching news may be decidedly unhelpful for your mental well-being. Checking Facebook for twenty minutes once a day to keep in touch with friends and family may be OK, but letting it disrupt your productivity at work or interfere with face-to-face conversations with people is unhealthy.

Decreasing negative input is only half the equation. Your mind needs positive input, and you're responsible for making sure it receives such. Think about how you learned to feed yourself when you were a child. At first you didn't have much choice about what, when, or how much you ate, but learning to feed yourself gave you much more control. Now that you're an adult, you can eat what, when, and how much you choose. You can do the same with your mental food. Consider things that you find mentally nourishing—uplifting media, time with positive family and friends, time in nature or solitude, or the spiritual food of God's Word. Look for mental food that provides encouragement, inspiration, positive education, helpful role models, relaxation, or spiritual ministry.

Learn to feed yourself—mentally. Thoughtfully choose
to take in high-quality mental nourishment such
as uplifting media, time with family and friends,
time in nature or in solitude, and God's Word.

I get scores of e-mails every day, but there are three specific e-mails I look for and enjoy every morning—e-mails from three ministries that I find nourishing and encouraging to my soul. You can do the same. The resources are endless. Choose high-quality mental food, and your thoughts will naturally improve.

CHOOSE WHAT TO THINK ABOUT

This is where you put into action Philippians 4:8—thinking about whatever is true, honest, just, pure, lovely, of good report, etc. The word Paul uses here, *logizomai*, is strong. I translate it as "continue to meditate on, focus your mind on, these things." It's a very active word, indicating focused and ongoing effort. It's just the opposite of letting your mind drift, thinking whatever thoughts present themselves.

When your thought habits are negative, fearful, anxious, worried, or—let's face it—lazy, making the effort to focus on the kind of positive thoughts Paul refers to may seem impossible. But it's not. Remember, the POWs who came through their experience unbroken were those who chose to focus on what was positive and on what they did have control over. It doesn't matter how bad your circumstances are; there are always positive things to think about.

Here are a few categories of good things to think about. Take some time considering each category, and see if there aren't some good things in your life in that category that you can focus your mind on.

- People you care about and who care about you. I find it hard to remain upset when I think about spending time with my four grandchildren. Your family may not be the ideal family, but they care about you. Think about the friends you have. Remember the times you felt close and happy with them.

- People you admire. Biographies of successful people, stories of people who overcame significant obstacles, people whose character you admire: role models such as these are a great foundation for good thoughts. Look for resources about them that can inspire your own life.

- Others who need help. Getting your mind off yourself is one of the best ways to lift your spirits and stop worrying. There are always people in need. Get involved in a cause you care about, such as a homeless shelter, a big brother or big sister program, improving literacy, rescuing abused animals, rescuing victims of human trafficking, or one of many others.

- What God has done. One of the most important benefits of my journal has been to look back and see where God did something wonderful for me. If you haven't previously done so, begin now to record what God does for you, and periodically go back and remember. Hearing what He's done for

others can also lift your faith and encourage you
that He can do the same for you.

- God's Word. Reading, meditating on, memorizing, and studying God's Word is the most
high-quality mental food you can get. There's no
excuse today for not getting regular input from
God Himself through the Bible. Subscribe to a
daily devotional e-mail based on God's Word,
install the Bible app on your smartphone and join
a daily reading plan, or join a small Bible study
group at your church. Fill your mind with nourishment from the Bible regularly.

Perhaps you're saying, "Do I have to do these things?" That
would be like saying, "Do I have to eat every day?" There's
nothing legalistic here. We're talking about good mental input
so that your mind can be resilient, positive, hope-filled, and fully
alive. It's not wrong to occasionally take in some pure entertainment any more than it's wrong to enjoy some ice cream occasionally. But if that's your steady diet, neither your body nor your
mind will be healthy. If you consistently feed your mind high-
quality nourishment, it may begin to taste like dessert.

CHOOSE WHAT TO THINK

We've talked about what to think about, you've paid attention to
the computer hardware of your brain and are giving your mind
high-quality input, but there is still another step: choosing the
software that determines how the input is transformed into the
output of thoughts, feelings, behaviors, and character.

The good news is that you can reprogram your computer, or
update your software so to speak. You can change not only what
you think about but also the actual thoughts you think about
those topics. The high-quality mental input you're now putting
into your mind will help you do this. This becomes especially
important when you truly must think about negative, hurtful,

or wrong things such as what you see in the news, a health or relationship challenge, or some other difficulty. Remember, godly thinking does not mean refusing to notice what's wrong. Read the Bible; much of it is about God's people who did wrong or experienced tragedies and then what God did in response to those circumstances.

Take charge of not only what you think about but also of the very thoughts you think about those topics.

Here are some positive characteristics to cultivate as you develop new thought habits:

- Consider the choices you have. You have options about how to respond to even the worst circumstances. If your job is too stressful, you can choose to set boundaries at work, look for a different job, optimize your stress-management outside of work, or develop your own business. If your spouse is ill, you can choose, instead of worry, to focus on finding the best care and join a support group. Your choices may not be the ones you want, but you always have choices.

- Grab on to joy and hope. You can acknowledge the worst while still placing your mental focus on things that are positive. When your finances are hit hard, be grateful for your health that allows you to look for other income. When a close relationship is broken, cling to the family or friends you still have. You can thoughtfully learn and grow your character from any difficulty.

- Take positive action. Your fear and anxiety will always lessen when you take action steps in a positive direction. You may not be able to change much, but focusing energy where you can take action will lessen your sense of hopelessness and improve your psychological well-being. It may not be easy; those actions may include changing your lifestyle, asking for forgiveness, getting some help, or participating in spiritual warfare.

• Determine God's view of your circumstances. Read His Word, pray, and get input from other godly people. Then think, speak, and otherwise focus on what God says about your problem. God may direct you to make some significant changes in your lifestyle or your thinking or to take some other action in cooperating with Him. When you've done what is in your power to do, remaining focused on His viewpoint helps you maintain a position of trust, hope, and resilience.

I challenge you to practice thinking in these ways. Speak them out loud when you're alone and to others. Write them in your journal. Your brain's computer software will update to run in a positive direction more naturally as you take these steps. And see if your feelings don't also change as you continue these thought habits.

TAKE TIME TO THINK

Sometimes life gets busy and we simply react to all the junk in our lives rather than thinking. On a regular basis—at least once a week—set aside some time for real thinking. Take an hour or so and go to a place where you'll feel calm and not be disturbed. Begin with prayer if you wish: "Lord, I'm afraid, anxious, and confused. I claim Your promise of a sound mind. Be with me right now. I ask for clarity and wisdom. Amen."

Give your emotions a little time to settle. Cry or beg or yell if you must. Then be quiet in His presence. Ask yourself the questions that come to your mind. Ask them of God. Write or speak out loud if you wish. Listen for what God has to say about your situation, and think about what your next steps in cooperating with Him might be. Simply getting quiet for the purpose of thinking may allow your mind to think things you've never thought before.

Regularly taking quiet time to think may be one of the best investments you can make in your personal well-being.

GETTING SOME HELP

Sometimes you need help to break unhealthy thought habits and establish healthier ones. Admitting you need help is not a sign of weakness; it may be the most courageous and healthy thing you can do. Thankfully there are many resources available today if you need some help in this area.

> At least once a week set aside some time to just think. It may allow your mind to think things you've never thought before.

Celebrate Recovery is a Bible-based fellowship of individual recovery support groups helping individuals with hurts, habits, and hang-ups in a confidential Christ-centered environment.[1] There's probably a group at a church near you. Having others to walk this journey with you can provide wonderful encouragement, balance, and support.

If you find yourself unable to choose your thoughts, and especially if you are troubled with thoughts of harming yourself or others or have difficulty staying in touch with reality, you may need professional help. Ask your friends, pastor, or doctor to suggest a Christian counselor or therapist in your area. An online search may give you more possibilities. If at your first or second appointment you don't feel this person can understand you or provide the help you need, look for someone else. You're not the first person to face struggles such as you have, and there are people who are willing and eager to help. Pray for God to direct you to the right person.

CHOOSING YOUR THOUGHTS

What you think about and the specific thoughts you think have a powerful impact on your well-being. While you have less control over your external circumstances, you have significant control over your thoughts. Pay attention to the input you allow into your mind, and make sure it will result in the outcome you desire.

Choose to focus your mind on things that meet Paul's filter in Philippians 4:8: whatever is true, honest, just, pure, lovely, of good report. While you cannot ignore problems, focus the majority of your mental energy in the positive direction. Choose to take charge of the specific thoughts you think about any problem. Focus on the choices you have, the actions you can take, and God's view of the situation.

QUESTIONS FOR CONTEMPLATION AND DISCUSSION

1. How many of your thoughts do you allow to come passively? How many of your thoughts do you take active control over?

2. What is the quality of the input you allow into your mind—from the people around you or from various forms of media?

3. Following the guidelines in this chapter, think about, talk about, or write about some positive thoughts you could choose regarding a current problem you have.

CHAPTER 5

THE ROLE OF YOUR LIFESTYLE

Y OU WOULDN'T THROW wood on a fire that you were trying to put out, would you? Trying to overcome fear and anxiety without addressing the factors in your lifestyle that are making them worse is just like that. You wouldn't consciously choose to live in a way that fuels your psychological distress, but you may be doing exactly that every day. It's not only what happens to us that may drive fear and anxiety; sometimes it's what we do to ourselves.

It may be uncomfortable to imagine that elements in your lifestyle may be turning you into your own worst enemy, but this is actually very good news. To whatever degree your lifestyle is causing or adding to your distress, you have the power to change its root causes and thereby experience wonderful freedom. This is not a blame game; it's both a sobering and an empowering exploration of a whole category of measures in which relatively small changes on your part may have very large consequences for your well-being.

When people hear the word *lifestyle*, they may get defensive or feel discouraged. You may think, "You're going to tell me to quit smoking and lose weight. I've tried that, and it doesn't work." Or perhaps, "I'm stressed, and I'm doing the best I can. Don't try to get me to change." I get it. I don't like people trying to tell me what to do either.

Me trying to push you into making changes you don't want to make will most definitely not work. At best you'll join a gym for two weeks, wear yourself out, and quit. Or you'll promise your spouse to leave work on time, and next week when your boss asks you to take on an extra project, you'll stay late again.

Lifestyle changes are often difficult. The only way you'll make such difficult changes is if you find your *why*. We'll talk about a number of lifestyle measures that will improve your fear and anxiety and bring you a sense of personal well-being, but first it's important to explore how you can tap into the motivation you'll need to stick with those changes even when you don't feel like it.

FINDING YOUR *WHY*

My husband, Al, said he didn't remember a time when he didn't smoke. After nearly fifty years, smoking was part of him. Even seeing his good friend die from the respiratory complications of smoking was not enough to get him to quit. When Al and I got married, he told me he finally had a big enough reason to go through the agony of quitting: he wanted to stay alive as long as possible to enjoy life with me.

Your *why* will be unique, but you must find it and hold on to it if you want to change. Simply hearing that people who sleep a certain number of hours each night are happier and healthier, or that you'll die sooner if you don't lose weight, is not likely enough to motivate you to stick with any changes long-term. You need a personal *why*, one that taps into your heart, that you can go back to when things get tough and that's bigger than the discomfort you'll feel in the early stages of change.

All change is hard. If the consequences of continuing your self-destructive behavior are bad enough—jail, bankruptcy, or hospitalization—the negative motivation is sometimes enough to overcome the roadblocks to change. If you're facing negative consequences because of your lifestyle, notice them, acknowledge the pain, and use it to begin the process of doing things differently.

Positive motivation is usually more powerful in the long run, however. Think of what it would mean if you could wake up refreshed in the morning with a clear mind, face the day with focus and energy, make a meaningful impact in the lives of others, and end the day feeling satisfied and hopeful. And think what your life could be if you experienced that kind of day over and over again. How different is that from the way you are living now? How could you then impact the people you care most about?

When finding your *why*, the more specific, the better. Here are a few things to consider as you think about what your *why* might be.

- The way you want to feel and live. You want freedom from your constant anxious thoughts and fearful feelings. You want to be able to engage in some specific activities such as travel, work, or ministry. You want to experience joy and peace instead of always being sick and tired.

- Your impact on the people close to you. A husband and wife I know well lost over one hundred pounds each because they wanted to actively engage in their children's lives as they grow up. Your love for a spouse, children, or close friend may provide you the necessary motivation to change.

- God's desire for you. I hope your relationship with God is intimate and strong. If so, knowing that He wants you to live in a certain way or make a change in your lifestyle is perhaps the best motivation of all. You sense in your heart that growing in such a way will make you more useful and effective in God's kingdom.

Whatever your *why*, think it through carefully. Make it as big and specific and positive as you can, remembering it is unique to you. Write it down, or perhaps find a picture that symbolizes your *why* and put it on your smartphone or your mirror.

Keep your *why* in front of you regularly, and it will help you be successful.

To make a difficult lifestyle change, find a *WHY* that
is big enough, specific, positive, and unique to you.

Now for some specific lifestyle areas that will help improve your psychological well-being.

THE FUEL YOUR BRAIN AND BODY NEEDS

It's time to think about providing your brain with a steady supply of the nutrition it needs and avoiding substances that may trigger psychological distress. That means paying attention to what you eat and drink.

What to eat

The neurons in your brain need the right supply of glucose—blood sugar—to function normally. Too little blood sugar and your brain will become sluggish and irritable, or worse. Too much blood sugar, such as in diabetes, can harm your brain cells in other ways. When you feel like reaching for a snack in the late morning or late afternoon, your brain may be sending a signal that its sugar supply is running low.

Our typical Western diet is full of processed carbohydrates that are quickly broken down and absorbed, rapidly raising blood sugar. Too often, however, your blood sugar crashes shortly thereafter, leaving you feeling irritable, tired, and possibly hungry again. Those rapid swings in blood sugar make it difficult for your brain to function well consistently. If you struggle to control your weight, this can be a factor causing you to consume more calories than your body needs.

The remedy is not counting grams of carbs, but ramping up the unprocessed foods in your diet. It's easy to understand that white sugar in desserts, sodas, and other foods gives you a blood sugar spike followed by a crash, but so does processed grain—refined flour. Most breakfast cereals, crackers, pastas, breads, baked goods, and snacks contain refined flour. Its effect on your body is almost the same as eating simple refined sugar.

Unprocessed carbs, on the other hand, affect you very differently. Vegetables, whole grains, and some fruits are processed by your GI system much more slowly, leading to a slower blood sugar rise without a crash later on. Regularly eating unprocessed carbs gives your brain a steady supply of glucose without the dramatic highs and lows that can be so damaging. When choosing vegetables and fruits, look for a variety of deep and bright colors. For vegetables, fresh is best, followed by frozen, and then canned. For fruits, fresh is best also. For canned fruit, look for varieties packed in natural juice rather than syrup to decrease the sugar content. Whole grains such as oatmeal or whole-grain bread can also be healthy. For detailed information on the way individual foods affect your blood sugar, check the glycemic index.[1] A lower glycemic index means that food raises your blood sugar less and would therefore generally be healthier in this regard. But don't worry about getting too technical; focus most on choosing more unprocessed foods.

Your brain also needs healthy fats and protein. These are also digested more slowly and may help you feel fuller longer. Again, go for unprocessed foods as much as possible; lean poultry and fish, nuts, legumes, or avocados are great. A well-planned vegetarian diet can supply all the protein and other nutrients a healthy brain needs. Limit or avoid fried or baked goods, cookies, desserts, or quick-prepare foods such as most frozen meals, processed snacks, or fast food; these are usually loaded with unhealthy fats.

The effect of milk products on your mental well-being is somewhat controversial. If you use a lot of milk products and struggle with fear and anxiety, try significantly cutting back or eliminating dairy products for a period of time and evaluate how you feel. A small group of people are sensitive to dairy products, and you may have to test yourself by eliminating them for perhaps a few weeks to know how they affect you.

What *not* to eat

The second part of the connection between diet and anxiety is eliminating substances that trigger psychological distress. The top of this list is food additives. Have you read the list of ingredients on boxes, cans, or packages of foods you buy? Ingredients include preservatives, coloring, flavoring, stabilizers—the list is long. God did not create your body to handle all those chemicals. If a food has a long shelf life or is ready to eat, it's probably processed. Some of the biggest culprits here include lunch meats, frozen dinners, packaged goods, candy, sugary drinks, and snacks.

The remedy, again, is unprocessed foods. To stay away from processed foods with harmful ingredients, buy most of your food from the periphery of the store—the produce section, the fresh meats, etc. The frozen section can be a good area as well (especially for fruits and vegetables), but be cautious to stay away from the processed foods there also. The shorter the list of ingredients on a package, usually the better. If it's perishable, it's likely less processed. A farmer's market is also a great place to find healthy, unprocessed foods.

I often get asked about organic foods. The preservatives and other chemicals in processed foods are clearly much more damaging to your health and well-being than nonorganic produce or meat. If you have eliminated all or most of the processed foods from your diet, but you still struggle with psychological distress and want to do more, going organic may help somewhat. Organic meat may make a bigger difference than organic produce. However, focus first on moving away from processed foods.

If processed foods have been a big part of your diet, moving to unprocessed may be a challenge. To begin, take one processed food each week and move to a less processed alternative. Here are a few examples:

- Instead of a frozen breakfast sandwich, choose fresh eggs and whole-grain toast.

- Instead of sugary boxed cereal, choose instant (or old-fashioned) oatmeal.

- Instead of fish sticks, choose frozen or fresh unbattered fish filet baked at home.

- Instead of chips or a granola bar, choose an apple or banana and peanut butter.

- Instead of a frozen TV dinner, choose home-cooked chicken stir-fry.

The closer you can get to God's green earth, the better. In our twenty-first-century culture that's not always 100 percent possible. Each step you move in that direction will help your brain—and your body—be happier. Making these dietary changes slowly will help you stick with them longer.

What to drink

Finally, what you drink is also important. Your brain is mostly water by weight, so you need lots of water every day. Sweetened or caffeinated beverages are not the answer. Because of their glucose content, you already understand how regular soda or fruit juice can create a blood sugar spike and then crash. Artificially sweetened beverages are at least as bad, if not worse. You should avoid artificial sweeteners if you struggle with psychological distress. These substances create an addiction-type response in the brain, making you crave more food—and sugar.

The caffeine in tea and coffee may trigger anxiety as well. Try going off caffeine completely for a period of time; if your anxiety decreases, you've made the right decision. If not, at least limit the use of caffeine to the morning hours, and in modest quantities, to help improve your sleep at night. Herbal teas (no caffeine) are a different story. Some may be calming and can be a great addition to your anxiety-reducing lifestyle.

Eating plan

Here's a simple eating plan that will be healthy for your body and provide your brain with the best possible support for thinking clearly and feeling calm.

Drink water, and lots of it. What's the best water? The kind you will drink! If you're not used to drinking water, try adding a slice of lemon, cucumber, or strawberry. Limit fruit juice to a couple ounces a day; the vitamins may be healthy, but juice raises blood sugar too rapidly.

Eat at least three meals a day, consisting primarily of unprocessed fruits and vegetables, lean unprocessed protein, and whole grains. Try to include protein with each meal; it will help you feel fuller longer and supply your brain and body with what it needs. If you feel you need snacks, plan ahead and make sure they're also unprocessed.

The topic of nutritional supplements is too large to cover in detail in this book. I can suggest a couple, however. There is some limited evidence that chamomile, lavender, and passionflower may be beneficial for anxiety. I often also recommend a phytonutrient supplement such as JuicePlus.[2] It has not been proven to improve mental well-being specifically, but it provides many nutrients in just the way God built them into nature. However, don't spend your hard-earned money on supplements until you have optimized your diet. That's where your health dollar will make the most difference right away as well as in the future.

SLEEP, SWEET SLEEP

If you struggle with fear and anxiety, sleep can be elusive. Worry can make it difficult to fall asleep, or it can wake you up during the night. The what-ifs, memories, or upset feelings keep your brain from being able to turn off and stay that way. You know that your brain works more clearly with enough sleep—which you can't get, so you worry more. It's a vicious cycle. Anxiety also keeps you from sleeping well, which makes you all the more anxious.

You won't die because you don't get a good night's sleep occasionally, but if you are sleeping poorly most nights, taking steps to improve your sleep will do a lot for your psychological well-being. Your brain will function more clearly and creatively after sleep, and you'll be able to handle your emotions and life's stresses with more resilience.

If you struggle with sleep, make sure you take the necessary steps to prepare your body, mind, and environment for sleep.

Preparing your body for sleep

There are several steps you can take that may improve your sleep.

Exercise.

A tired body will fall asleep easier. That is an important benefit of physical exercise for anyone, but especially for those who struggle with fear and anxiety. Exercise improves your sleep in several ways. Stress increases certain hormones in your blood such as cortisol, adrenaline, and others. Thirty minutes of physical exercise most days will "use up" those stress hormones, causing your body to desire restoration—sleep. After exercise, your muscles relax more easily, you will feel less tense, and you will naturally fall asleep easier. Exercise itself will lessen your anxiety, and it also helps eliminate other toxins and chemicals from your body that can prevent you from relaxing.

Strenuous exercise late in the evening may not be wise if you struggle with falling asleep; it may take a few hours for the "worked up" feeling to dissipate. Exercising in the morning, or at least as soon as you get off work, may be best. Thirty minutes of vigorous walking or jogging, cycling, or an aerobic workout at least four days each week will make a big difference in both your physical and psychological well-being. Some people find that exercising regularly is sufficient to improve their sleep and cure their psychological distress. What exercise is best? The kind that gets your heart rate up—and the kind that you will continue doing!

Thirty minutes of moderate exercise most days each week will…

- "Use up" stress hormones in your body
- Promote physical and mental relaxation
- Improve your physical and emotional well-being
- Improve your sleep

Watch your diet.

Eating late at night may keep you from sleeping well. Give your stomach three to four hours to digest the bulk of your evening meal before trying to lie down. If you need a bedtime snack, keep it light and stay away from refined carbs. Keeping your body and brain "clean" by limiting processed foods will also improve your sleep.

Look for sleep apnea symptoms.

Watch out for signs of sleep apnea. If others tell you that you snore or gasp during the night, get checked out. Morning headaches or dry mouth, daytime drowsiness, and trouble concentrating are other common symptoms. Losing weight (if needed) and specifically treating the sleep apnea will do wonders for your sleep—and for your psychological well-being.

Assess medications and supplements.

Medications and supplements may affect your sleep. Talk with your doctor or pharmacist about whether any of your medications or supplements may be contributing to your insomnia. Don't consume anything containing caffeine after noon; caffeine remains in the body much longer than most people realize. Research on how supplements such as melatonin, valerian, chamomile, and lemon balm affect sleep is controversial. Check with your doctor before using any supplement long-term.

Should you try over-the-counter or prescription medication for sleep? Although not technically a sleep aid, Benadryl helps some people sleep and may be relatively safe for most people and is available without a prescription. Prescription sleep aids are not a good answer for more than a few nights, however, and should only be used in extraordinary circumstances. There is a real risk of dependency or addiction, and the sleep they induce is different from the natural sleep your brain and body need most.

Follow a sleep schedule.

Go to bed and get up at approximately the same time each day, weekends included. That habit will help your brain get accustomed to when sleep is appropriate. A short nap—twenty minutes or so—during the middle of the day can be very helpful; longer naps will likely make it difficult to sleep at night.

Preparing your mind for sleep

Starting an hour or so before bedtime, take measures to get your brain ready for sleep.

Only allow calming input late at night.

Instead of watching TV, try listening to calming music, reading a book, or taking a warm bath. Read one or more of the Psalms or other favorite Bible passages. Such input will help slow down your mind and prepare your brain circuits for sleep. Right before bed is not the time to bring up a painful subject with your spouse or begin working on something stressful, such as your budget.

Put away worries and anxieties.

When you begin turning off entertainment and other stimulation, your mind may start to worry and wonder and try to figure things out—and before you know it you're all upset again. Try the technique of putting your fears, worries, and other anxious thoughts somewhere external to you. Visualize a box on the shelf or dresser. As you go to bed, mentally take each worry out of your mind, look at it for a moment, place it in the box, and then close the lid. All your worries will be there for you to pick up again tomorrow if you need to. You might also write down any concerns or ideas; then your mind can relax without having to worry about forgetting anything important.

Claim God's promises for restful sleep.

The Psalms have some wonderful passages you can meditate on as you prepare your mind for sleep:

> I will both lie down in peace and sleep; for You, Lord, make me dwell safely and securely.
> —Psalm 4:8

> He will not let your foot slip; He who keeps you will not slumber. Behold, He who guards Israel shall neither slumber nor sleep.
> —Psalm 121:3–4

> It is in vain for you to rise up early, to stay up late, and to eat the bread of hard toil, for He gives sleep to His beloved.
> —Psalm 127:2

Out loud, place your worries, fears, stress, or anxiety in God's hands, and ask Him to give you rest. You can know that He will be caring for you even as you sleep.

> To sleep better:
> - Stop the mental stimulation an hour before bed
> - Visualize putting your fears and worries in a box on the shelf, and close the lid
> - Claim God's promises of restful sleep

Preparing your environment for sleep

The physical characteristics of your surroundings may make a big difference in your sleep.

If your bed or pillow is uncomfortable, investing in a replacement may significantly improve your sleep. Playing white noise such as recorded nature sounds, a fan or soft motor, or very soft calming music may help. Make the room as dark as possible; for some people even the small LED lights on electronic devices may decrease sleep quality.

Pay attention to the temperature in your sleeping area. Most people sleep best when the room is between 65 and 70 degrees. A room that's too warm or too cold may cause you to wake up frequently. Try adjusting the temperature until you find where you sleep best.

Your goal is not to eliminate stress. Your goal is to learn how to make stress work for you rather than against you.

If you struggle with getting adequate sleep, limit any activities you might normally do in bed (except intimacy with your spouse, of course). Don't watch TV, work, or talk with friends on the phone in bed. Your brain will get the message that when you go to bed, it's time to sleep.

If all these measures don't result in reasonably good sleep most nights, and you're still anxious, consider an evaluation by a sleep specialist. Doing so may improve your quality of life in many ways.

STRESS

Is there anyone who can honestly say he or she doesn't have stress? And you really wouldn't want to be completely stress free; the only people without any stress at all are dead people! The most successful athletes, businesspeople, and creatives have discovered how to use stress to their advantage. They may invite "artificial" stress, such as deadlines, goals, or competition. They have learned how to harness that stress to maximize their performance and accomplish things the rest of us look at with envy. Think of the people you admire most; many of them likely have taken unbelievably stressful circumstances and turned them into a platform for personal growth and for ministry to others.

Instead of eliminating stress, your goal should be to make stress work for you rather than against you. Unmanaged stress is a huge source of fear and anxiety. As with your physical health and your thinking, you need to learn how to take charge of your stress.

Manage stress wisely.

You will be able to manage a lot more stress than you ever thought possible if you remember two things: you always have more choices than you think, and your "stress muscles" will strengthen as you alternate periods of exertion with periods of rest. Let's look at each of those ideas.

You have choices.

We talked a lot about taking control of and making choices about what you think about. This is an extension of that principle. Think about what is causing you the most stress right now and what choices you may have in that area. Here are a few examples:

- You're short on money. Your choices could include scrutinizing your budget for areas where you can save, saying no to things you might normally do, requesting overtime at work, asking for a raise, starting a side business, or taking a class on financial management.

- You're short on time. Your choices could include asking for help, saying no to requests for your involvement, quitting some activities, or choosing to lose sleep temporarily while you take steps to adjust your schedule in the future.

- You hate your job. Your choices could include investing time and energy outside of work in things you enjoy, looking for another job, working to change the conditions at your office, starting your own business, or learning ways to find fulfillment in the work you are doing now.

- Your marriage is in trouble. Your choices could include reading books or listening to podcasts on how to have a healthier marriage, asking an older couple with a successful marriage for help, leaving the marriage (as a last possible resort), getting help from a marriage counselor, or going on a weekend marriage retreat.

Any choice you make will have consequences, some much larger than others. Realizing that you have choices will empower you and put you in a healthier frame of mind.

Alternate stress with rest.

The second idea is that of alternating stress with rest. You know this principle from physical training; gradually increasing the distance you run or the weight you lift will strengthen your muscles and cardiovascular system as long as you allow adequate time for rest in between periods of exercise. Stress management works the same way. You can't work on your grief, addiction, troubled marriage, childhood abuse issues, or any other anxiety-producing challenge continuously. You'll burn out.

Instead, intentionally look for ways to find rest and renewal as you work on your challenges. What works best for you will depend on your personality and on the type of stress you're under. Think of moments in the past when you felt alive, joyful, energized, or at peace, and find more opportunities to feed your soul in those ways. Spending time in nature, reading a good book, listening to or creating music, being alone doing nothing, exercising, spending time with friends or family, and spending time with God may help you. As you need to learn to feed your mind nourishing mental food (see chapter 4), you need to learn to feed your soul nourishing food also. No other human being or institution can do that for you.

Ideally you'll find ways to nourish your soul on a daily and weekly basis, as well as a few more dedicated times throughout the year. That could mean a five-minute walk during your break at work or reading a book for twenty minutes before going to bed. You might reserve one evening a week for time with friends in a small group. A couple times each year go on a weekend retreat through your church or a short getaway with your spouse. Find what brings you peace or joy, and do more of that.

Types of stress

Now let's look at three common areas that cause people stress: money, time, and people.

Money and stress

In a recent survey 72 percent of people stated they were stressed about money.[3] Dealing with significant debt, an income that doesn't meet basic needs (not wants—needs), having a different financial personality from your spouse, having no savings to deal with the unexpected, an illness that brings large medical bills and/or prevents you from working—these and other money matters are certainly reason for stress.

Remember that you always have choices. You can decrease your money stress. Intentionally set in place a process by which you tell your money where to go rather than wondering where it went. Crown Financial Ministries and Financial Peace University are high-quality, Christian-based organizations that offer many resources to guide you through these principles if you need help.[4]

God cares about your money and your money stress. Choosing to place your money under God's control is an important stress reliever; that's what stewardship is. For the believer stewardship is not really about giving money to your church, although that may be one piece. It's about acknowledging that God has something to say about whatever resources you have—finances included—and He wants to help you learn how to use them wisely so both you and others will be blessed.

Time and stress

Time is one of the few truly nonrenewable resources, and you, I, and everyone else on the planet have exactly the same quantity to spend each day. It's easy to allow time pressures to rob our peace. Habitually running late for work or appointments, overcommitting to organizations or people, trying to involve your children in every available extracurricular activity, agreeing to participate in events or activities that are outside your true priorities—these are just some of the time habits that lead to stress and anxiety.

I'm a performance-oriented person, and I often believe I will be able to accomplish something in less time than it actually takes. I've had to discover that my worth and success are not dependent on how fast I run. I've had to learn to work smarter rather than harder by concentrating on what is most important rather than what is simply urgent.

If time stress is difficult for you, begin by looking at the way you spend your time as a matter of stewardship. Set a process in place in which you dictate how your time is spent rather than wondering where your time went. Ask others to help you spot time wasters. Learn how to say no to activities or commitments that don't line up with your true priorities.

People and stress

People will drive you crazy! At least they will if you let them. Everyone has an idea of what you should be doing with your family, money, time, and life. Some people seem to make your life difficult simply by their presence in it.

Remember you have more choices than you realize. It is OK if some people don't like you; some people will, and some people won't. How freeing to finally come to the realization that you don't have to please everyone! Your stress level and your effectiveness in life will improve greatly when you learn to live your life before an audience of One—God Himself. That's a biblical principle as well (Gal. 1:10).

Learning to say no to people is hard. Learning to not worry about what other people think is hard. I know—I had to learn those things. It will feel very uncomfortable at first, but the lower level of stress you experience after learning to do so will be worth it. Remain as true to your purpose as you know how to be, and ask God to continue to make that clear to you.

YOUR LIFESTYLE AND ANXIETY

Not all psychological distress is caused by what happens to you; sometimes it's what you do to yourself. Your lifestyle contributes a great deal to your psychological well-being. Finding a personal *why*, a motivation, that's big enough to withstand the difficulties of change will help you be successful in improving your lifestyle.

Eating a diet based primarily on unprocessed food and plenty of water will provide your brain with the fuel it needs to function well and will limit many substances that may trigger fear and anxiety. Working to prepare your body, mind, and environment for restful sleep will improve that important anxiety-reducing part of your daily life.

Stress happens to everyone. You can manage much more stress than you realize by paying attention to and acting on the many choices you do have regardless of your circumstances and by intentionally finding opportunities to feed your soul in nourishing ways.

QUESTIONS FOR CONTEMPLATION AND DISCUSSION

1. What is the quality of nourishment you are providing your brain? Do you need to make any improvements in your eating or drinking habits?

2. How are you sleeping? When it comes to preparing your body, mind, and environment for sleep, what one thing do you think would make the biggest difference for you?

3. What is the most stressful circumstance you are facing right now? What choices might you have in how you respond to that very circumstance?

CHAPTER 6

THE SPIRITUAL ROOTS OF FEAR AND ANXIETY

H OW DID WE come to be like this? Have you ever thought about that? In so many ways both society at large and our own personal lives bear only a slight resemblance to how God originally intended us to be and live. We are too often broken, sick, and miserable. That may sometimes be the case even for those of us who are committed believers in Jesus.

The daughter of a colleague of mine was in some serious trouble. She approached the world with a dark and angry heart. Her parents' breakup and the hurtful behavior of Christians around her had turned her against God and Christianity. She started moving from one destructive relationship to another, and she became involved in the occult in what she saw as the only way to find meaning.

My heart ached for her. My colleague and other Christians had pounded her with "truth" repeatedly, but she only put up more walls and moved further into her world of darkness. I wanted to take her by the shoulders, look into her eyes, and say, "You don't have to live like this!" But my colleague moved away before I could develop the kind of friendship with her daughter that would have allowed me to speak into her life in such a way.

I think God feels that way about us sometimes. We hold on to our wounds, our destructive behaviors, our insistence on doing life our own way, and our world continues to become darker as a result. God sometimes has to find a way to pull us up short and shout, "You don't have to live like this! You don't have to hurt yourself and everyone else. Let Me show you another way."

That's a picture of sin, and it causes us trouble—sometimes right away, sometimes in the future, and sometimes in ways we don't even realize. God cares enough to try to prevent us from experiencing the suffering that sin will bring.

Sin is not some arbitrary concept dreamed up by a punitive God looking for a way to make us miserable. Sin is failure to live life God's way. Sometimes it's overt acts that go against His laws. Sometimes it's failure to do things He directed us to do. Sometimes it's our internal rebellion even when we may externally try to comply, such as Jesus talked about in the Sermon on the Mount. (See Matthew 5.) Sin is a politically incorrect topic in our culture, but how it affects us has not changed.

What does sin have to do with psychological distress? Everything. When our lives are out of alignment with God and His plans for us, fear and anxiety are a natural result. It may be God's way of shouting, "You don't have to live like this!" It is also a symptom of the larger sin problem—the cosmic conflict between the kingdom of God and Satan's kingdom of darkness. As we look at the possible spiritual roots of psychological distress in this chapter, I pray God opens your mind and heart to see where this may apply to you.

DOING SOMETHING WRONG?

All sin can mess with your mind and set you up for fear and anxiety. Some habitual sins do this exponentially. Having a marital affair; being addicted to gambling, pornography, or spending; and constantly having to cover your lies with more lies—the natural consequences of such sins cause plenty of fear and anxiety. There's the fear of getting found out, the fear of not being able to quit, and the fear of God. Those fears may be legitimate. But thank God there's a way out!

God's primary goal for you is not your comfort. He's bigger

than that, and His plans for you are too glorious for Him to be satisfied with you only being happy.

Imagine you're a classic car enthusiast. One day you discover your dream—a 1957 Chevy two-door hardtop. It's broken down: the leather seats are torn, the body is rusted, and the engine hasn't turned over in years. You love the car, so you pay the price and trailer it to your workshop. But you also love it too much to leave it in that broken-down condition. You immediately set about tearing down, sanding, painting, repairing, and replacing— restoring it to the glorious specimen you know it can be.

You and I are not unlike that broken-down Chevy. God loves us the way we are—"big" sins or "little" sins—but He loves us too much to let us remain in our broken-down condition. He may have to put us through some very uncomfortable sanding, tearing down, and replacing for us to be what He knows we can become. And when He's done, we will be an example of the glo-rious work that He can do with a human being who is totally devoted to Him.

We can make that restoration process easier or harder. We may fear opening up those painful wounds—perhaps for good reason— but our resistance intensifies the pain. We may not understand which dysfunctions are caused by others' behavior toward us and which are caused by our own choices, but God knows what steps we each must go through to reach that final goal.

When Israel resolutely refused to respond to God's calls for repentance, God promised to make things very difficult for them. "I will hedge up your way with thorns, and make a wall, so that she will not find her paths" (Hos. 2:6). It wasn't because He desired to cause them pain; He was shouting, "You don't have to live like this!" He did whatever He could to get them to listen, respond, and come back. "Therefore, I will allure her, and bring her into the wilderness, and speak tenderly to her" (v. 14).

He created you in His image, as His child, to be with Him, talk with Him, understand Him, and join with Him in having dominion over this part of His universe. The sinful nature we inherited, the sins that are done to us, and the sin we engage in ourselves are so contrary to God's creation that feeling uncomfortable—fearful or anxious—when we act or live contrary to His plan is, in some ways, part of our very nature.

As with the Israelites, however, we may become rebellious and hardened. If necessary God may make us very uncomfortable as He attempts to get our attention and bring us back to Himself. If you have never made Jesus Lord of your life, the Holy Spirit may use every discomfort possible as He works to open your eyes to truth and bring you into God's kingdom.

Does God cause us pain? Does He inflict trauma, tragedy, or sickness on unsuspecting humans in order to get His way? The reality of evil—both in the world and in our lives—can only be understood in light of the battle between God and Satan, and we'll talk more about that later in this chapter. As far as sin in our own lives is concerned, the Bible presents God as a loving parent, using every means possible to bring us to maturity. "God is dealing with you as with sons. For what son is there whom a father does not discipline?" (Heb. 12:7).

But I don't feel like it's wrong.

Perhaps you've avoided the idea of sin, or you're uncomfortable and wonder whether something you're doing is sin, even if you don't think it's wrong. How do you know?

Religious people and institutions have a tendency to come up with lists of outward behaviors that you're supposed to do and not do. The Jews in the Old Testament were very good at that, and God did not look kindly on that behavior: "For I desired mercy, and not sacrifice, and the knowledge of God more than burnt offerings" (Hos. 6:6). The Pharisees in Jesus's day were also good at that, and He quoted that same Old Testament scripture in rebuking them: "But go and learn what this means, 'I desire mercy, and not sacrifice.' For I have not come to call the righteous, but sinners, to repentance" (Matt. 9:13). Outward behavior matters, but God's larger concern is the state of your heart.

So then does anything go as long as your heart is right? That's certainly what culture supports, but that's not what God's Word says. Truth is not whatever you want it to be. The Bible presents God's way as right and every other way as wrong. The problem is human beings tend to add on their own regulations to what God desires.

How are you to differentiate between what God desires and what human beings might say? That's where the Holy Spirit comes in. Isaiah promised, "Your ears shall hear a world behind you, saying, 'This is the way, walk in it,' whenever you turn to the right hand and when you turn to the left" (Isa. 30:21). The New Testament quotes God's promise through Ezekiel in saying, "I will put My laws in their minds and write them on their hearts" (Heb. 8:10). The Holy Spirit will make clear what is sin and what needs to change for the person who is listening.

When the Holy Spirit puts His finger on something in your heart and says, "This right here; it needs to change," and you refuse to listen, it becomes sin.

Many experiences—including our own decisions—may deaden our ability to hear the Spirit's voice. No one can play junior Holy Spirit in another person's life. That doesn't mean pastors don't have a responsibility to teach about sin, or that you and I have no responsibility for speaking into another person's life when God gives an opportunity. But we must remember that it's the Holy Spirit's action in each person's heart that counts, not our words. God does the saving, convicting, and changing.

When it comes to your own heart, natural human tendency is to say, "I'm OK. The Holy Spirit hasn't talked to me about this, so it's not sin for me. So don't you talk to me about this either!" That's a very dangerous place to be. God may use people to help you understand what sin is and what you need to change. But remember that something is sin because of what God says about it, not because of what other people say about it.

People frequently ask whether a certain behavior is sin. "Is it a sin to smoke or drink alcohol?" Or, "How far can I go sexually with my girlfriend before it becomes sin?" One thing is clear: once the Holy Spirit puts His finger on that place in your heart and says, "This right here needs to change," and you refuse to let it go, it is sin. It may be an outward behavior or it may be an attitude of the heart. That's the point at when God's discomfort may set in. You may feel all kinds of distress until you agree with what the Spirit is saying, repent or change your direction, and do it God's way.

Will you comply perfectly? Probably not. Who of us can? But that's why God promised to write His laws in our hearts (Heb. 8:10). The longer and more attentively you listen to Him, the quicker you comply with the Spirit's prompting, the easier the process will become, and the more like Him you will be. You will more easily recognize His voice and experience more peace.

The Holy Spirit doesn't dump on you the whole list of things you need to change all at once. It's a process. There will be easier and harder times, periods of quicker and slower growth. Give God permission to be in charge of your spiritual maturity, and He will not let you down!

Forgiveness is not enough.

When I was a tween, I became very concerned about my standing with God. I believed in forgiveness, but I was afraid that I would forget to confess some sin and end up missing heaven. Every evening I would write down a list of anything I had done wrong. Then I meticulously asked for forgiveness from God and anyone else I might have wronged. I wrestled with the shame of confessing to anyone, but my fear kept me doing so.

I've grown a lot since then. If I do something wrong, I still ask for forgiveness from God and anyone else who may be affected, but I no longer live in fear. I'm confident and settled in my relationship with God. Much of that growth has come from learning that forgiveness is not enough. Forgiveness deals with our past; we also need something that deals with our future.

Jesus came to deal with both our past and our future. His life, death, and resurrection take care of both. Yes, we have a clean slate. He has bought and paid for our broken-down-'57-Chevy selves, and we belong to Him. But until and unless we allow Him to restore us, we remain broken, afraid, and anxious. His forgiveness never goes away, and we will continue to need it as long as we live. But we need His healing, transforming power in our lives just as much.

I'm praying that you are miserable right now—at least about the things you need to change. I'm praying that even as you read this, the Holy Spirit is putting His finger on something in your life and saying, "This right here—I want this. Let me change you here." I pray you quickly surrender that specific thing, whatever it is. God is big enough, good enough, and loving enough to change you in the place you are most ashamed of. Surrender does not mean white-knuckling it in order to do the right thing. It means letting go of your own way, giving God permission to change you from the inside out, and cooperating with Him.

Do you want peace instead of fear and anxiety? Let God have His way with you. Until then, "the wicked are like the troubled sea when it cannot rest, whose waters cast up mire and dirt" (Isa. 57:20). But when you do, "those who love Your law have great peace, and nothing shall cause them to stumble" (Ps. 119:165).

Divine discontent

There's another time when God wants you uncomfortable—not afraid or especially anxious, but discontented. We can easily get stuck in a rut, continuing to do things in our personal life, family, work, or ministry just as we've always done them. We may not be sinning or doing anything specifically out of God's plan, but God knows there's something better available for us, and He doesn't want us to miss it.

When the children of Israel had been "comfortably" moving around their area of the wilderness for a long time, God said to Moses, "You have circled this mountain long enough. Now turn north" (Deut. 2:3). It was time for them to move toward taking the land of Canaan that God had promised them.

Sometimes God stirs things up in order to move you forward

so you can experience His best. He may make your external circumstances uncomfortable or orchestrate a level of divine discontent in your soul. Not every feeling of dissatisfaction is divine discontent, and you can't blame God whenever something starts to feel difficult. But as you come to know the Lord better and better, there will be occasions when He makes you unsettled in order to get you to follow Him to the next place He has for you.

God is not likely to push you forward in this way if there are areas of your life that you have not turned over to Him. If the Holy Spirit is convicting you and working to change some area of sin or immaturity in your life, deal with that first. But if you don't believe that's the case, feel unsettled, and wonder whether it's divine discontent, here are a few questions to ask yourself and God:

- Have I become too comfortable with what God has been doing in and through me up until now?

- Is there a dream in my heart that has not yet been fully accomplished?

- Has God given me gifts or resources that are not being fully exploited for His kingdom?

You may not immediately know what direction God is directing you to go. Be patient. Spend time in prayer over days, weeks, or longer. Give God permission to make Himself clear to and to stretch you. The door that opens may not be simple or easy, but you will have an inner sense of peace when you begin to step forward into the new thing God has for you.

DOING SOMETHING RIGHT?

Jesus promised His disciples serious trouble. He was inviting them into a life of opposition, want, persecution, perhaps death—and peace. "I have told you these things, so that in me you may have peace. In this world you will have trouble. But take heart! I have overcome the world" (John 16:33, niv).

How would you have responded if you had been there and

heard Jesus's promise of trouble? It's easy for us to look back and say we would have followed Him too, but can we really be sure? What if your whole life was turned upside down, your family disowned you, you had to leave your home, and people were constantly out to kill you? There are places in the world where those are the consequences of following Jesus today.

And you thought your reasons for fear and anxiety were bad enough!

Sometimes doing exactly the right thing brings the most serious trouble. And you don't always know in advance what kind of trouble, if any, doing the right thing will bring.

Jesus promised His followers—and us—trouble because of the larger context in which we are living. The only way our lives really make sense is to see them as part of the larger drama of the conflict between God's kingdom of light and Satan's kingdom of darkness. If you picked up this book looking for a discussion of spiritual warfare, this is what you've probably been waiting for.

Here's the short version: The battle between good and evil is real. Jesus has won. Yet we are still caught in the cross fire. It's as simple—and as gloriously terrible—as that.

But remember that in the very same statement that Jesus promised His followers trouble, He also promised them peace. Understanding this war, your place in it, and the victory available to you will help you experience that peace in both the fear and anxiety you may feel about natural things and within warfare in the spiritual realm.

To use our broken-down-'57-Chevy analogy, God didn't call you, save you, and transform you in order to put you in the garage and keep you shiny. His goal is not to put you in a car show, polished and pretty. His goal is to enter you in the race to end all races, one that the whole universe will be watching. He not only enters you in the race, but He also expects you to win. You will never be alone; His presence will be with you every step of the way.

The battle between good and evil is real. Jesus
has won. We are caught in the cross fire. It's as
simple—and as gloriously terrible—as that.

Isn't that a glorious thought? It's been your destiny ever since your creation, and especially now that you have aligned yourself with God and His kingdom.

But being on God's side, being restored and entered in the race to end all races, puts you at odds with God's enemy. And that's where you may experience serious trouble.

The dangers of spiritual warfare

Surviving, let alone winning, this war would be completely hopeless on your own. God's enemy—and yours—is cunning, wise, and strong. When Satan attacks you, it's because he hates God and the damage you can do to his kingdom of darkness as a follower of Jesus. Some Christians have come to think of spiritual warfare as simply a better technique or stronger weapon with which to fight the devil. If that's all it is, friends, then you and I are toast! Some believers have picked up some spiritual weapon and marched out swashbuckling against some spiritual enemy and ended up badly bruised and broken. Please don't do that!

If the question in the great conflict between good and evil was about who was stronger—God or Satan—the contest would have been over a long time ago. God could have easily destroyed the devil and those angels who aligned with him when He cast them out of heaven (Luke 10:18). Spiritual warfare is not about mustering up some magical spiritual strength in order to win.

While discussing techniques of spiritual warfare, some will be tempted to focus on the techniques themselves. Seeing spiritual warfare as a method to solve your problems can become dangerous. If you focus primarily on the power that Jesus has given believers over the devil and his kingdom, you're missing the point. Jesus said, "Do not rejoice that the spirits are subject to you, but rather rejoice that your names are written in heaven" (Luke 10:20).

This is not about you suddenly becoming strong enough to go out and fight the devil. Jesus already did that at the cross; you don't have to do it again.

Talking about spiritual warfare can also quickly deteriorate into toxic religion that can be damaging, especially when it comes to psychological distress. If you practice some spiritual warfare and it doesn't solve all your problems right away, you can feel as if you're right back where you started. Remember that Jesus promised us both trouble and peace (John 16:33). We can expect both trouble and overcoming in this life.

What God *has* promised is that we can live fully alive—in every aspect of our lives (John 10:10). This will involve God growing your character, which may sometimes feel uncomfortable. It will involve Him stretching you to become more than you thought you could be and you being poured out in meaningful service for something bigger than yourself. You are being prepared for eternity!

The answer to the dangers of spiritual warfare as a method is to focus not on the war, but on Jesus. Spiritual warfare is never an end in itself. It's a way of understanding the realities that God has revealed about His grand scheme and where we fit into it.

Along the way you will experience brokenness and healing, sorrow and joy, tears and gladness, weakness and strength. You will experience what feels like temporary defeat and failure, but you will also experience true victory and success.

What is spiritual warfare?

This question is best answered by looking at what the whole cosmic war is over. Remember, if the fight was over power or territory, we wouldn't be in this mess. God's power would have done away with evil a long time ago. "The earth belongs to the Lord, and its fullness" (Ps. 24:1).

This war is about allegiance. It's about your heart and mine, and the heart of every other human being. It's much more helpful to see our situation as a love story. Yes, a love story.

Think of your favorite fairy tale, or perhaps movie or novel.

Those archetypes often express, in part, eternal truths; that's why they have such consistent and ongoing appeal. Think *Swan Lake*, or *Shrek*, or *Rapunzel*. Think *Gone With the Wind*, or *Casablanca*, or *West Side Story*. And you could probably name a dozen more.

These famous story lines usually include at least a hero, a heroine, and a villain. The questions intrigue us: Will he get the girl? Will she recognize her hero? Will she know how much he wants her? Will she give her heart to the villain? The hero often has to wage war against "the world, the flesh, and the devil" in order to prove his love to his beloved and rescue her from certain death or some other terrible fate.

But there is no point unless he can win her heart.

You, my friend, are the point of the story. It's you He is waging war to rescue. It's you He is desperate to prove His love to. It's your heart He seeks to win.

The war between good and evil, God and Satan, is not about power or territory. It's about your heart—your love, allegiance, and worship.

All the techniques and methods and prayers and Bible verses and psychological insights in this or any other book about spiritual warfare are pointless if Jesus does not win your heart. It's your allegiance that both God and the devil are fighting for. Remember that Jesus won the war against Satan not by force, but by love.

So don't see yourself as a little Christian warrior out there on your own, or even with some of your buddies, simply searching for some better ways to fight the villain in your life, happy enough to win a few more battles here and there. Yes, we'll talk about some of those ways to win battles, but if that's your primary takeaway, I will have failed.

Instead, see yourself as a fought-for and delivered royal member of the bride of Christ, being prepared to rule with Him for eternity. Your allegiance is firm. Your heart is won. You are completely on His side—now and forever. Whatever the villain brings against you will fail because your heart is steadfast. Now you can join with Jesus in extending His rescuing, delivering, healing, wooing influence into other hearts that are broken and defeated.

The greatest evidence that God is true and that Satan is defeated is you—your life, completely transformed into Christ's likeness, firmly planted in the kingdom of God, unmoved by the convulsions this world goes through as it nears the end of the age.

That's what spiritual warfare is really all about. That's what it means to be more than a conqueror (Rom. 8:37).

What does spiritual warfare have to do with fear and anxiety?

There are at least two ways spiritual warfare may add to your psychological distress as a Christian: the topic itself and experiencing attack.

First, the topic itself: using terms such as *battle*, *victory*, *enemy*, and *weapons* sounds violent. And indeed it is. Just read the Bible; there's plenty of violence there! War may naturally breed fear and anxiety. If you focus on the fight, you'll probably feel more upset rather than less. I'll even show you research to prove that in the chapters ahead.

How do you overcome this? Make sure your focus is not on the battle, but on Jesus. Thinking about the devil too much can actually give him more power in your life. Jesus never looked for a fight with Satan. One large part of His ministry was "healing all who were oppressed by the devil" (Acts 10:38). His focus was not on the devil, but on doing the will of His Father. That's where you need to focus too.

Another way in which spiritual warfare may be affecting your psychological well-being is the possibility that your mind itself may be under attack from the enemy. I want to be very careful here. I do not believe that every time God's children feel anxious or afraid that it is because Satan is trying to plant thoughts in their heads. There are several other possibilities, as we have already discussed.

But sometimes such distress is caused by a direct attack from the kingdom of darkness. When that happens, Jesus has made available a pathway for you to be free. It's not magic; it's part of the restoration He wants for all His children. And this book will help you along that journey to wholeness that He died to make available to you.

SOMETHING WRONG OR SOMETHING RIGHT?

If doing something wrong and doing something right can both result in psychological distress, how do you know which it is? Do you need to repent and work with God to change your heart or your behavior? Or do you need to sing "Onward Christian Soldiers" and get to work moving forward?

It may not always be either/or; it might be both. The Holy Spirit will not stop working on your character as long as you're on this earth, and Christ's victory is available to you whatever level of spiritual maturity you have or have not developed. But if you're in a season of trouble, here are some questions that may help you discern what God is trying to have you understand at this time.

- Are you aware of something in your life that the Holy Spirit is trying to change?

- Is there any resistance in your heart to doing what the Spirit wants you to do?

- Are you taking every action step you are aware of to move forward out of this trouble, such as changing your lifestyle, taking control of your thoughts, investing in healthy relationships, and spending time regularly in God's presence?

- Have you taken time to thoughtfully and prayerfully seek God's perspective of your situation?

- Have you sought input from sources such as Scripture, godly friends, church leaders or counselors, or Christian literature?

- Have you evaluated your situation in light of what you know of God's plan for you, taking into account factors such as unselfishness, forgiveness, courage, peace, love, and joy?

- Is what you're attempting to do in life or ministry based on what you want or what you truly believe God wants?

- Is there any place in your soul where you sense a measure of God's peace? What action would you take from that place?

Prayerfully and thoughtfully contemplating these questions can help you see what God would have you do. God doesn't often show you the entire path in front of you. But He has promised to be with you and to show you the next step you need to take. And when He shows you that next step, be ready to move forward.

SPIRITUAL REASONING FOR FEAR AND ANXIETY

Sometimes our fear and anxiety stem directly from spiritual roots. When we're doing something wrong—sinning or living in some way displeasing to God—our peace is broken. God's restoration process, His ongoing work to transform us into His likeness, may feel uncomfortable. The Holy Spirit will ask to change you. When you agree and work with Him to change, your peace will be restored.

Sometimes we're doing something—or many things—right, and trouble comes. This spiritual warfare is not about you as a believer becoming strong enough to fight the devil; Jesus already did that. It's about the battle for your heart. When your heart is settled, nothing the enemy can do will move you. Techniques of spiritual warfare can make you wiser and stronger, but they are never an end in themselves. The focus must remain on Jesus, and then you will experience His victory.

QUESTIONS FOR CONTEMPLATION AND DISCUSSION

1. Is there an area in your life right now where the Holy Spirit is saying, "This right here; I want this!" Have you been resistant? Are you willing to let Him change you?

2. What are some ways in which you have experienced God's transforming work in your life, mind, and heart? How are you different now than when you first believed?

3. Do you sense that you are experiencing psychological distress as a direct result of the enemy's attacks? Have you experienced any victory there?

PART II

WHAT THE BIBLE SAYS

Therefore do not worry about tomorrow, for tomorrow will worry about itself. Each day has enough trouble of its own.
—MATTHEW 6:34, NIV

Be strong and courageous. Do not be afraid or dismayed, for the LORD your God is with you wherever you go.
—JOSHUA 1:9

So we may boldly say: "The Lord is my helper; I will not fear. What can man do to me?"
—HEBREWS 13:6

CHAPTER 7

"BE ANXIOUS FOR NOTHING"

C AN YOU IMAGINE Jesus ever being anxious? He carried the destiny of the whole world on His shoulders. From the moment of His birth He had enemies who were out to trap, discredit, and even kill Him. And yet He was not uptight, worried, or anxious about His material needs, the responses of the people around Him, facing the devil, or accomplishing His purpose in saving the world.

That doesn't mean Jesus didn't have feelings and temptations. We know Jesus can sympathize with all our struggles. He "was in every sense tempted like we are, yet without sin" (Heb. 4:15). He felt hunger, fatigue, pain, anger, weakness, and sorrow. He faced the same temptations we do: greed, lust, bitterness, and the urge to distrust His Father. He faced determined opposition from men and from Satan himself. Yet He was not anxious.

And we are told to have the same attitude: "Be anxious for nothing" (Phil. 4:6). If God told us to do so, then He must know we can comply. As with all God's commands, we can't comply perfectly immediately just by wishing to do so. It takes understanding, growth, and God's work in our hearts to achieve that result.

So let's look at what Jesus and others in the New Testament had to say about anxiety and how we can experience freedom from anxiety in our own lives.

WHY YOU SHOULD NOT BE ANXIOUS

Being anxious doesn't make sense. It's unwise and harmful. Perhaps your rational mind already knows anxiety is usually irrational and counterproductive, but your feelings don't want to comply. Examining your underlying beliefs and making sure they are consistent with what God says is an important step in bringing your thoughts and feelings into alignment with God. Jesus knew that as human beings we are prone to worry and anxiety, but you don't have to remain stuck there.

The first and perhaps most important reason of all to not be anxious is because that's what God has asked you to do. In one sense it's simply a matter of obedience. Thankfully there's also a lot more in God's Word to help you understand why—and how. And keep reading; we'll soon get to the practical steps of how you can accomplish this.

Worry won't change anything.

Anxiety is borrowing tomorrow's troubles for today. Jesus said, "Therefore do not worry about tomorrow, for tomorrow will worry about itself. Each day has enough trouble of its own" (Matt. 6:34, NIV). A big reason not to worry is that doing so will make absolutely no difference in the outcome.

Consider the thoughts running through your mind when you're anxious. Do they sound anything like this? "What will we do if I don't get this job? We won't have enough money to live on." "I've never done this before, and I'm not sure I can do it. If I fail, everyone will think I'm stupid." "This pain is getting worse. I must have cancer or some other terrible disease." "Spending this holiday with my family is going to be horrible. Everyone will be watching for me to mess up." You could probably name many worrisome ideas rumbling around in your anxious mind.

But ask yourself, has worry ever once improved the outcome of whatever situation you're in? Frequently our worst worries don't come to pass anyway. But even if they did, has your anxiety ever made things better? Jesus said that by worrying you can't add one inch to your stature (Matt. 6:27). I learned a long time ago that worrying won't increase my vertically challenged height of nearly five feet by one iota! And my angst didn't add one moment to my husband's life.

It's not that God doesn't understand your worry; He does. But anxiety doesn't help. It uses up energy for no reason and gets you nowhere.

Worry chokes your spiritual life.

The next reason you shouldn't be anxious is that it stunts your spiritual growth and blocks a deeper relationship with God.

Think of your very best human relationship. Perhaps it's with your spouse, a parent, or a very close friend. You know everything about each other, and you can trust this person completely. If you don't have that kind of a relationship, imagine it. Can you imagine being anxious about your relationship and trusting the person at the same time? Probably not. The more you know this person, the more your trust grows. There's no space for anxiety between you.

Just so, anxiety and worry impede your relationship with God. Worry constantly looks inward. Your focus is on yourself and you can't hear anything else, not even what God is trying to say to you.

Jesus talked about the different kinds of people who hear the Word of God. Those who "are choked by life's worries" were never able to grow (Luke 8:14, NIV). They did not spiritually mature or become fruitful; the message from God had no effect. Worry and anxiety keep you from growing in your ability to trust God, and they stunt your entire spiritual life. That's not the kind of life you want or that God wants for you.

Worry is unnecessary: God's got this.

The final big reason not to worry is that God has it covered. Your anxiety won't make Him work differently or more quickly. Resting in trust is the appropriate response.

There's a whole section in the Sermon on the Mount in which Jesus talks about how unhelpful it is to worry about material things such as food, clothes, and life on the earth (Matt. 6:25–43). My paraphrase: "Why do you spend time worrying about comparatively insignificant things? God takes care of the birds and the grass; don't you think He will take care of you too?" The King James Version says, "Take no thought…" (v. 25). In other words, don't even think about it! "Your heavenly Father knows that you have need of all these things" (v. 32).

Many years ago when I was facing some serious financial problems, I remember reading this chapter in Matthew over and over again and seeing, "Don't even think about it!" Perhaps that message will speak to your heart in your own worries as well.

Does God follow through on His promises? David said, "I have been young, and now am old; yet I have not seen the righteous forsaken, nor their offspring begging bread" (Ps. 37:25). God has all the material resources in the world and all the human resources imaginable at His disposal, and He can direct them your way. He has specifically promised you strength, encouragement, and direction that only the Holy Spirit can provide. He is an inexhaustible source of everything you need—now and forever. When you need something, ask Him. "Be anxious for nothing, but in everything, by prayer and supplication with gratitude, make your requests known to God" (Phil. 4:6). And God's response? "My God shall supply your every need according to His riches in glory by Christ Jesus" (v. 19).

As you contemplate how completely God has promised to take care of you, be sure to put this in the context of Scripture as a whole. These promises don't mean you will automatically have everything you want or that you won't have struggles. Timing, God's greater purpose for you, and the facts of our sinful world are part of the equation. The point is that worry is worthless because God's got this!

Trusting God with our needs does not mean we can become lazy. God told Joshua to get up because there was work to be done. (See Joshua 7:10.) Some interesting research demonstrates what this looks like. When faced with serious problems, people generally relate to God in one of three primary ways: some try to handle things on their own, some sit back and wait for God to deal with it, and some see themselves as working together with God in every way they can. Those in this third group, who collaborate with God in dealing with their problems, generally come through those challenges with the best physical, emotional, and spiritual well-being.[1]

This idea goes along with the World War II chaplain's encouragement to his men; "Praise the Lord and pass the ammunition!" Action plus trust—it's the best combination.

BIBLICAL STEPS TO GETTING PAST ANXIETY

So you should not be anxious, but how do you do that? It's one thing to know what you should do; it's quite another to do it successfully, especially when this involves so many emotions and subjective feelings. When anxiety has become your default way of responding to life or challenging situations, you need something more than "don't do it."

Sometimes Christians feel guilty when they can't immediately comply with what God asks. Your guilt over your inability to not feel anxious may just make you feel all the more anxious! Let me reassure you that Jesus knows how you feel. There are many steps along a journey such as this, including dealing with the issues of physical health, lifestyle, and thinking. What's important is that you work with God and continue to take steps toward accomplishing this.

In many ways anxiety is like darkness. You can't eliminate darkness from a room by trying harder. You can only make it undark by bringing in light. In the same way, you'll only overcome anxiety by putting something else in its place. That means eliminating root causes and proactively learning to trust God. The Bible gives several steps that will help you do just that.

"Think on these things."

In chapter 4 we talked about how important it is for you to take control of your thinking. Remember, you have the ability to choose your thoughts. Paul makes it explicit: "Finally, brothers, whatever things are true, whatever things are honest, whatever things are just, whatever things are pure, whatever things are lovely, whatever things are of good report, if there is any virtue, and if there is any praise, think on these things" (Phil. 4:8).

This scripture applies to overcoming anxiety in at least two ways. First, it speaks to the kind of input you allow your mind to take in. Some people build you up and some people tear you down. Some media are uplifting, godly, and faith friendly, while other media are discouraging, sensational, and ungodly. You have a choice about the mental food your mind receives. Choose that mental nourishment that will help you grow and become stronger personally, mentally, and spiritually.

Second, this scripture speaks to what you actively choose to focus your mind on. When anxious thoughts and worries present themselves to your mind, you don't have to give in to them. You can actively replace those anxious thoughts with ones that are based on what you know about God and His Word.

Here are a few examples:

- If your finances are in trouble, your anxious thoughts may sound like this: "I'm stuck in this never-ending place of poverty. No one, not even God, is helping me, and it's hopeless. If this continues, my family and I are going to end up homeless. I'm a failure, and God doesn't care." You can replace those thoughts with something like this: "My financial situation is serious. God knows that, and He cares about my family and me. He has promised to care for us like He cares for the birds, and I choose to trust Him. I will pray for God's direction and provision as I continue to work hard to find or create the income our family needs."

- If you or a loved one is sick, your anxious thoughts may sound like this: "I'm never going to get well.

God is punishing me because of my unhealthy lifestyle. I'll never learn how to deal with all this medical stuff, and nobody cares enough to help me. I might as well give up." You can replace those thoughts with something like this: "I may have contributed to my illness by my lifestyle, but that means I can contribute to my getting well by changing what I can. I will keep on praying for God's healing, knowing He is with me whatever happens. I'm going to cooperate with Him and with the medical professionals to get as healthy as I can in order to serve God the best I can."

• If you struggle with some habitual sin or addiction, your anxious thoughts may sound like this: "I'm a failure. Nothing I do will make it any better. All I do is hurt those I care about. This Christian life just doesn't work for me, and God can't do anything about it for me anyway." You can replace those thoughts with something like this: "Yes, I've hurt myself and others. But God has promised me forgiveness, a new beginning, and a good future. I'm going to get the help I need, and I'm going to humbly ask God to take this part of my life and change me. I'm going to learn all I can about applying Jesus's victory to my own life and continue to walk forward one day at a time."

Replacing anxious thoughts with positive thoughts does not come easily. That's why it's important to spend time with other growing believers and in God's Word. Doing so will help counteract the negative messages your mind naturally grabs onto. Do that long enough, and your anxious feelings will give way to the empowering light of God's truth.

Focus outside yourself.

Anxiety and worry are quite selfish. Anxiety keeps you from being useful and productive for yourself, your family, and ultimately God's kingdom. The antidote is moving your focus outside yourself. It's hard to stay upset when you're truly focusing on helping someone else.

It's difficult to remain anxious when your thoughts and energies are focused on helping others for God's kingdom.

Perhaps the very best place to direct your focus outside yourself is to God's kingdom. In His discussion of anxiety in the Sermon on the Mount Jesus said, "Seek first the kingdom of God and His righteousness, and all these things shall be given to you" (Matt. 6:33). To whatever degree you understand God's purpose for you, direct your physical, mental, and spiritual energies in that direction, and you won't have nearly as much left over to devote to worrying.

You may think you don't understand much of God's purpose for you, but it is not some big ethereal grandiose position at some point in your future. God's purpose for you starts where you are now, and that's where you should begin. These questions will help you take some of those next steps in fulfilling God's purpose for you:

- What aspects of your character is the Holy Spirit working on? (See Romans 8:29.)

- Who has God placed around you who needs to experience His love? (See John 15:12.)

- What resources—material things, knowledge, skills, abilities, interests, connections—do you have that you can invest for His kingdom? (See Romans 12:6–8.)

- Whose need breaks your heart? Whose pain do you feel? How can you help?

You will experience moments of exhilaration as you invest all you have for God's kingdom, whether in your own home and family, in business, in charity work, or in His church. There will be times when you feel as though you're riding a wave of God's making as you join Him in His work. And that focus drowns out anxiety.

Practice gratitude.

Gratitude is something you can choose, and it's one of the best antidotes to worry and anxiety. "In everything give thanks, for this is the will of God in Christ Jesus concerning you" (1 Thess. 5:18). Having gratitude is part of taking control of your thoughts and choosing where you focus your mind.

We're talking about spiritual warfare in this book, and that means we have to be honest about the very real effects of evil. How can we be grateful when we look at ISIS terrorism, human trafficking, diseases such as cancer, and political upheaval, let alone the problems in our own lives? Those whom Paul asked to be grateful were experiencing "these afflictions" and "tribulation" too (1 Thess. 3:3–4). Gratitude in the midst of unspeakable trouble doesn't come naturally, but God asks it of us.

Recently I listened to a widow speak about God asking her to be grateful shortly after the death of her husband. She asked, "God, how can I be grateful for losing my husband?" God's answer to her was, "I didn't ask you to be grateful for his death. I'm asking you to be grateful for him—for his life, for the life you had together." In whatever circumstance you find yourself, you can reframe your thinking to find something for which you can be grateful.

What might that look like? If you just lost your job, be grateful you still have your health so you can look for another. If you are a caretaker for a sick loved one, be grateful for another relative, friend, or respite care that provides you a break on occasion.

If you are struggling with health problems, you can be grateful for God directing you to helpful professionals. If you are struggling with PTSD, addiction, or abuse, you can be grateful for the moments of clarity in which you can feel God's peace and see bits of His direction for your future.

God always has a way of bringing something good out of what the enemy meant for harm (Gen. 50:20). That doesn't mean we will not suffer. But God can turn what you thought was hopeless into bread by which you can feed others who need hope and help. And you can always be grateful most of all that you know Jesus who has been victorious over evil and that you know how the story ends.

Enter His rest.

Have you ever worked hard to rest? It seems counterintuitive. But that's what we are told to do: "Let us labor therefore to enter that rest" (Heb. 4:11). This again is a conscious choice we must make to stop trying to figure out things beyond our control and let God handle it.

There are several aspects of choosing rest, and we can think of them as entering into rest in the dimensions of spirit, soul, and body.

Body

When it comes to physical rest, sleep can seem elusive if you struggle with anxiety. Review the discussion about sleep in chapter 5 if you need to and follow its steps accordingly.

Beyond sleep, your body needs rest from constant productive activity. Long work hours, endless activity, and back-to-back events will take a toll on your well-being. This kind of lifestyle over a long period of time will damage your health and your relationships and lead to other regrets. No one on their deathbed wishes they had worked longer hours. Take the time to think through your priorities and consciously schedule time to invest in the people you care about, or to just *be*.

Soul

Your mind, your soul, also needs rest. If your days involve intense creative work or focused mental activity, rest may simply mean putting a limit on the number of hours you exercise your mind in that way. Physical exercise, time in nature, or time with family, friends, or church groups can be restful. Look for places, people, or activities that fill you up, and consciously go there regularly. Healthy play—doing things just for fun and enjoyment—can be very refreshing.

Spirit

Your innermost being, your spirit, needs rest too. The message of the gospel is not, "Do this." When Jesus said "It is finished," it meant the work is done (John 19:30). You don't have to struggle or try to make God love you, to find out what He wants for you, or to become good enough. The most important things are already accomplished by Jesus Himself. Your role is to rest in that completed work. Give God control of your spiritual growth. Tell Him out loud, "Lord, I give You permission to grow me, to change me. I ask You to be in charge of bringing me to be who You want me to be. And I will cooperate with You in every way I can." He's able to finish what He started in you: "Being confident of this, that he who began a good work in you will carry it on to completion until the day of Christ Jesus" (Phil. 1:6, NIV).

Cast your care on Him.

One of the strongest passages in the New Testament about spiritual warfare comes in 1 Peter 5:8–10, and we'll explore that more in the chapters ahead. But immediately before that, in verse 7, Peter says "Cast all your anxiety on him because he cares for you" (NIV). The Greek here paints a very colorful picture of taking what you have and throwing it over onto something else.[2] It's the same word used to describe the way Jesus's disciples threw their garments on the donkey that He rode into Jerusalem (Luke 19:35).

You cannot fight the devil from a position of worry and

anxiety. Before you pick up any weapons of spiritual warfare, take a good look at your worry. Imagine it as something tangible, like a garment you're wearing. What are the thoughts and feelings it encompasses? What experiences may have led to your anxiety? What possible outcomes are you concerned about? Get it outside yourself and make it an object. Write it down or draw a picture if you wish.

And then do just what that verse asks you to do. Picture in your mind taking off that garment of anxiety and throwing it onto Jesus. You may need to do so over and over again until it becomes a habit. You might put this scripture on a card taped to your mirror or as the wallpaper on your smartphone so that whenever you begin to worry, you'll be reminded to take off that garment of worry and throw it onto Jesus.

You might also do something physical to symbolize casting your worry on Jesus. Take what you wrote or drew, crumple it up, and then tear it up, burn it, or throw it away. If your church has an altar, take what you wrote or drew and leave it there.

Don't get stressed out if these actions don't completely and forever eliminate your anxiety. Keep doing it if you need to, and it will help you experience the Holy Spirit's healing in your soul.

Let God handle the results.

Finally, there's no need to hold on to anxiety about anything God has asked you to do. If you are serving Him, there will be times—perhaps many times—when you will face opposition or even persecution. Other people won't understand and may openly try to stop you. Circumstances will make it seem as though your efforts are achieving nothing. Satan himself may stir up opposition as your work for God's kingdom damages his own kingdom of darkness.

Don't let those things concern you. It's human nature to want to see results, to understand beforehand what to expect, and to be assured of success. But often God asks us to step forward even when we don't know what the results will be or when we know those results will include trouble.

Jesus said to His disciples, "But when they deliver you up, take no thought of how or what you will speak. For it will be given you at that time what you will speak. For it is not you who speak, but the Spirit of your Father who speaks through you" (Matt. 10:19–20). Jesus didn't say to be unprepared, but to not worry. Our job is to follow His leading to the best of our ability and leave the results to Him. He will make Himself responsible for the results and for taking care of us even if we face opposition for doing His work.

Perhaps the best way to encapsulate what we're saying about worry and anxiety is to remember again the Serenity Prayer: "God, grant me the serenity to accept the things I cannot change, the courage to change the things I can, and the wisdom to know the difference. Amen."

NO MORE ANXIETY

Remaining anxious or habitually worrying about things is not what God wants for you. The New Testament makes it clear that you are to be anxious about nothing because it doesn't change the outcome, it harms your spiritual life, and God has promised to take care of you always.

The New Testament also provides steps by which you can overcome anxiety and worry. Those steps include taking control of your thinking, focusing outside yourself and on God's kingdom, practicing gratitude, and choosing to find rest for your spirit, soul, and body. In your imagination, or symbolically, take your anxiety and worry and throw it onto Jesus. His shoulders are big enough to carry it—and you.

QUESTIONS FOR CONTEMPLATION AND DISCUSSION

1. Are you worrying about anything that you cannot change? How has that affected you?

2. What thoughts could you choose to think in place of your worrying?

3. What would it mean for you to cast (throw) your worry onto Jesus?

4. Write or draw something that symbolizes your worry; then throw that paper into a river or leave it at the altar at your church to symbolize casting your worry onto Jesus.

CHAPTER 8

"BE NOT AFRAID"

W HEN I WAS a little girl my parents bought Bible story books for my sister and me. I can vividly remember the depiction of Jesus in the boat on the Sea of Galilee as the storm arose and threatened the lives of all aboard. When the disciples woke Him, Jesus stood up in the boat and with only a word calmed the wind and the waves. Then He looked at His disciples and said, "Why were you afraid? Why were you afraid when I was with you?"[1] (See Mark 4:36–41.)

Indeed, why are we afraid when He is with us?

In the Bible we are told "fear not" or "be not afraid" nearly one hundred times. God must have known fear would be a problem for us. He knows we are human beings, and fear is one of those emotions that seems to arise unbidden. It feels out of our control, but if God asks us to not be afraid, He must also know that getting there is something we can accomplish.

Fear is frequently a bedrock emotion underlying worry and anxiety. As you take the biblical steps discussed in the previous chapter to overcome those mental/emotional habits, you may discover a deeper level of fear in your soul that you didn't know was there. Those steps are still vitally important, but there's still more that God's Word has to say about overcoming fear.

Let's look at some biblical examples of when God said "Don't be afraid," and you'll find your own fear draining away. As with worry and anxiety, you can't fight fear by simply trying harder to not be afraid. The space that emotion occupies in your soul needs to be refilled with something stronger, something deeper, something more encompassing. And we'll find that in God's Word.

GOD'S PEOPLE WHO FACED FEAR

If you're struggling with fear you're in good company. Some of God's best friends were afraid; that's why He needed to say "Fear not!" so often. Joshua struggled with fear over the coming battles to take over the land of Canaan (Josh. 1:9). Elijah struggled with fear when Jezebel threatened to take off his head (1 Kings 19:1–3). David struggled with fear of his many enemies (Ps. 56:1–4). Jeremiah struggled with fear of what people would think of him (Jer. 1:8).

You may have heard sermons about overcoming fear based on Job 3:25: "For the thing which I greatly feared has happened to me, and that which I dreaded has come to me." Some have interpreted this to mean that if you are afraid of something, your fear will cause that thing to happen. That belief may have stirred up even more fear in your heart: "I'm not afraid. *I'm not afraid!* I'M NOT AFRAID!" God is not asking you to work yourself into a frenzy trying to not be afraid. There's a bigger picture of what the Bible says about fear that you need to understand.

The initial emotion of fear is not the problem; however, when you park there and let fear continue to have control, you suffer a negative impact on your well-being and dishonor God. Remember, you can't get rid of darkness by trying to push it out; you must turn on the light.

One of God's own, Peter, went from fearful to fearless. When Jesus first called Peter to follow Him, Peter was an uneducated fisherman accustomed to a hard life. During the three years he spent as Jesus's disciple and constant companion, Peter's mouth and impetuous spirit sometimes got him into trouble. Then, when Jesus was on trial just before His crucifixion, Peter denied Him three times. (See John 18:15–27.) We know that story, and like Peter, we may either say, "I'll never deny Him," or live in fear that we might.

Imagine things that night from Peter's perspective. The Jewish authorities arrested his leader, and the outcome wasn't looking good. His world and everything he believed appeared to be collapsing around him. He couldn't tear himself away from the spectacle but was afraid that if others recognized him they might arrest him also. His very life was at stake.

Did Peter have another option besides denying Jesus that night? Of course! But appreciate for a moment the very human fear going through his mind. I doubt you've felt any more afraid than Peter did that day.

But just a few weeks later everything about Peter was different. He and John ministered healing to the lame man at the temple gate. A crowd gathered in amazement, and Peter was soon speaking to them all about Jesus—apparently not caring what anyone thought (Acts 3:10–11). When Peter and John were soon arrested and called to stand before the authorities, Peter held nothing back. Even the authorities were surprised. "When they saw the boldness of Peter and John and perceived that they were illiterate and uneducated men, they marveled. And they recognized that they had been with Jesus" (Acts 4:13).

But Peter and the others weren't satisfied. When the early believers gathered together after Peter's and John's release, they prayed for even more boldness: "Now, Lord, look on their threats and grant that Your servants may speak Your word with great boldness" (v. 29). More boldness? There's absolutely no hint of the previous fear in Peter's heart. And the following chapters of Acts show that this prayer was fulfilled. Peter continued to preach Jesus right under the noses of those who would do anything possible to stop him and the others.

That freedom from fear stuck with Peter. When the Jewish authorities couldn't stop him, the secular authorities tried. Herod killed Peter's fellow disciple James and planned to kill Peter, but even that very real threat couldn't make Peter afraid. The night before Herod was planning to bring Peter out for public execution, Peter was so fast asleep in the prison that the angel sent to rescue him had to shake him awake (Acts 12:6–7). Could you sleep that soundly if you knew that you were about to be killed? Peter had truly overcome fear.

Peter's transformation demonstrates that even if fear has controlled you and caused you to do destructive or sinful things, you don't have to stay that way. The part of your heart that lives in fear can be healed and set free, and through God's grace you can develop courage and boldness, becoming fearless even in the face of the worst that the enemy can bring against you.

How did Peter get there? It wasn't by trying harder. It was through spending time with Jesus, seeing Him alive after His resurrection, and experiencing the Holy Spirit's presence. (See John 21:15; Acts 2:14–18.) It can be the same for you.

FEAR OF COMING TROUBLE

Our world is in trouble, and we know it. Terrorist attacks both in the Middle East and at home threatening the destruction of other nations demonstrate how vulnerable our society is. If you believe in global warming, then you believe our very way of life is putting our future survival at risk. News reports about the dangers to our food supply, water supply, and energy supply can sound like doomsday. Nuclear holocaust, monetary collapse, drug-resistant superbugs, and catastrophic natural disaster do not sound like far-fetched ideas.

Add to that the "softer" issues we see—the decline in society's acceptance of Christianity; controversies over such things as contraception, abortion, LGBT and gender issues; extreme political divisions; human trafficking and sexual exploitation; violence and sex in popular media; and the high rates of families torn apart by domestic violence, fatherlessness, divorce, single parenting, and poverty. It's unlikely you have read through these two paragraphs without feeling a twinge in your own soul about one or several of these problems that touch you personally.

Jesus predicted trouble, and He predicted our natural human fear response. "People will faint from terror, apprehensive of what is coming on the world" (Luke 21:26, NIV). Things will get so bad, Jesus said, that people's hearts will be "failing them for fear" as they look at what is happening around them (Luke 21:26, KJV). We need not be surprised when fear arises in our own hearts. Our world is groaning.

But for the believer there is no need to remain fearful. We don't just have the facts as we see them on the news, the Internet, and with our own eyes. We also have something greater. Whether or not society around us collapses because of monetary problems, rampant disease, terrorism, or extreme persecution, we know the greater truth. Jesus said, "When these things begin to happen, look up and lift up your heads, for your redemption is drawing near" (Luke 21:28).

IS FEAR EVER A GOOD THING?

As much as we read about "fear not," there is another dimension to what the Bible says about fear. The Old Testament describes it as "the fear of the LORD." Without fail, this is described as a good thing. Those who fear the Lord can expect life, wisdom, and all kinds of positive results (Prov. 9:10; 14:27).

In the New Testament Jesus echoes the same idea. In giving His disciples instructions prior to sending them out on their first missionary journey without Him, He alerts them to the opposition they will meet. But that opposition is not to be their concern. "Do not fear those who kill the body but are not able to kill the soul. But rather fear Him who is able to destroy both soul and body in hell" (Matt. 10:28). And that One is God, who holds their eternal destiny in His hands.

You've heard the fear of the Lord described as respect, and that's quite true. But the word *respect* doesn't go far enough, at least not in the way we usually think of respect. That would be an appropriate word to describe how you should relate to someone in authority such as your pastor or government leaders (Rom. 13:7). But God is in a whole different category. When we talk about God, we're not talking about someone you can negotiate with, someone who is just one or two steps ahead of you, someone you can match wits with, or someone you can get what you want from if you just play your cards right.

When you take time to contemplate who God really is, *respect* is just too tame a word to describe our response.

Who is your God?

We sing "How Great Is Our God," but we too easily forget how great He really is. He's not great because we can get Him to do what we want; He's much too big for that. We're talking about the Creator of the universe, the One who holds trillions of stars in the palm of His hand and at the same time holds the particles in each atom together with what scientists call "strong nuclear force."[2] (See Colossians 1:17.) Give all the credence you want to secular physics, but we are either an accident that defies belief or our God is greater than our wildest imagination can conceive.

It's even more amazing that our God became a man. In one indescribable moment the seat at the right hand of God the Father suddenly became empty. The One who had spoken galaxies into existence was now a human embryo in Mary's womb. Can we even begin to comprehend what it meant for Jesus to empty Himself of everything and become a human being, and then to die on a cross (Phil. 2:6–8)? Indeed, be astonished! But He didn't stay dead; He rose again and is alive forevermore. And if you were to see Him with your human eyes right now, you would be so overwhelmed that you would fall at His feet as though you were dead (Rev. 1:17).

But there's still more. This God who formed the universe and holds everything together by His power; who came to the earth in the person of Jesus to live, die, and live again; who ascended again to heaven and who sits at the right hand of the Father in unspeakable glory—this very same Jesus wants to come and live in you through His Holy Spirit! He's not only in heaven, but He is also very present in your life and mine. He sees you, knows you, understands you, loves you, desires you, and rejoices in you.

He is with you right now, closer to you than the very air you breathe.

When you truly know how great God is, you become
unafraid of anyone and anything lesser.

So next time you pray, remember that the One you are praying to right now, who is with you in the person of His Holy Spirit, is also the One who is risen from the dead and is gloriously alive, seated next to our Father on the throne of the universe.

We need to regularly be reminded of who our God is. This is who we worship and pray to. We are prone to making God into our image rather than allowing Him to re-create us in His image. When we forget this bigger reality, we may try to control Him or use Him for our own purposes, and He's simply too big for that.

This kind of a God might terrify you if you thought He was against you. But He's not. The good news of the gospel—indeed the whole Bible—is that He is for you. The truth of who God really is impacts our fear when we realize that He is on our side. Standing in awe of Him, how can we fear anything or anyone else? When you truly know how great God is, you become unafraid of anyone and anything lesser. "The Lord is my helper; I will not fear. What can man do to me?" (Heb. 13:6). Awe and worship are perhaps a better definition of "the fear of the Lord."

What difference does the kind of God you believe in make?

Considering what kind of God you serve is not simply an academic theological exercise. What you think, know, and believe about God has a dramatic impact on your psychological well-being. For a number of years Baylor University has conducted an extensive ongoing survey of religion in America. Their data show that people who believe in a punitive God—that God is out to punish you if you do something wrong—have significantly more psychological symptoms than those who believe in a benevolent God—that God is good and that He is on your side.[3]

Once you see the bigger picture of who God is, you have a choice in how you respond. You can shy away, put up your internal walls, and keep trying to figure out and control things yourself. If you've been trying to do that, let me quote Dr. Phil: "How is that working out for you?" Perhaps you've done pretty well for a while, but if you're like me, continuing to try to do things on your own just ends up in greater frustration, anxiety, and fear.

The alternative is not to cower in terror of God, but to let go. Here's a news flash: God is God, and you are not! There are things you don't know, things you don't understand, and things you can't change on your own. Voluntarily laying those things at Jesus's feet both releases their hold on you and gives God greater freedom to do things His way in, for, and through you. That's what Peter meant when he said, "God resists the proud but gives grace to the humble. Humble yourselves under the mighty hand of God, that He may exalt you in due time" (1 Pet. 5:5–6).

This scripture immediately precedes the command to "cast all your anxiety on Him," and then Peter's discussion of resisting the devil (vv. 7–10, NIV). You can't fight the devil from a position of fear, and the way to not be afraid is to choose to let God be in control. That doesn't mean you are passive; we'll talk a great deal in the coming chapters about your active role in the process. But it all begins with letting God have His rightful place in your heart, mind, and life.

If you're not sure that God is on your side, it's time right now to make things right between you and Him. You can't make yourself good enough to have God on your side. That happened when He came to the earth in the person of Jesus and died for you. Whether for the first time, or if you need to reconnect with Him, you can pray this right now:

Dear Jesus, I need You to be both Savior and Lord in my life. Forgive me for trying to do it on my own. Thank You for being my God. Amen.

"Fear God and give Him glory" (Rev. 14:7). Let the God of the universe be God in your life. And be eternally grateful that that very God is on your side.

STEPS FROM FEAR TO FREEDOM

But what can you do about your fear? Perhaps you're afraid of something "small" such as not finishing an assignment on time, making something new for dinner that nobody will like, or sharing your questions with your Bible study group. Perhaps you're afraid of something "big" such as dying from the same kind of cancer your mother suffered from, your marriage being destroyed by infidelity or anger, or a job loss threatening your family's future. Or perhaps you have been eaten up by fear for so long you don't know any other way to live, such as from PTSD as a result of child abuse or domestic violence, or an all-consuming fear of what other people will think.

Yes, you're afraid. And God said to not be afraid. How do you do that?

Let's look at three biblical principles that will help you overcome fear regardless of how large or small that fear is.

Learn, and then take action.

Sometimes information itself can diffuse a significant part of your fear. Your fear about an exam turns into confidence when you have adequately studied and prepared. Your fear of cancer may diminish greatly when you learn that a healthy lifestyle will decrease your risk of cancer by about half.[4] Those cancer risks are decreased even further if you maintain a lifelong mutually monogamous relationship and limit overexposure to the sun. Your fear over your marriage collapsing can resolve when you learn healthier ways of dealing with old baggage and managing conflict.

There's a certain amount of power that comes with knowledge. The first action step to take is to learn all you can about what you're afraid of. If it's fear of a specific illness, don't assume there's nothing you can do; find out any lifestyle measures or medical interventions that can lessen your risk or improve the outcome. If it's fear of public speaking, join Toastmasters, an organization that teaches public speaking, or find someone who's already a successful speaker to coach you along the way.[5] If it's a more global fear related to past traumas, read about people who have successfully moved past their trauma and what steps were helpful for them.

God often requires us to take action when we face problems, including fear. It's important to remember that our faith should not be in our actions; our faith is in God. Our actions are part of cooperating with God in moving toward the outcome He has for us. They are not guaranteed to prevent or solve our problems. Sometimes the most important actions we take are to adjust our attitude, thinking, and focus. But overcoming fear is not passive.

After you've learned all you can about the thing you fear, it's time to take another action step. At some point you'll need to do what feels scary even though you're afraid. Don't wait until you feel no fear; taking an action step forward is often one of the best ways to move past that fear and experience confidence. Those action steps may be small at first, but they are vitally important.

Your action steps might look something like this:

- Finding a recipe and buying the ingredients to make a healthy meal of unprocessed food

- Writing a clear but calm letter to your spouse expressing your thoughts and feelings about a serious conflict in your marriage

- Asking for help to set up a budget as you learn to manage your finances

- Compiling a list of twenty companies you could work for and sending your resume to the first three

- Getting three of your friends to listen as you
  practice a five-minute speech

Sometimes your most important action step is asking for help. Having a caring friend listen to your fear and be with you as you take those early action steps can be helpful. Especially if your fear is a response to serious trauma, having some godly professional therapy may be necessary. If you aren't making progress on your own, please ask for help.

Perfect love casts out fear.

There's no more powerful way to dispel the darkness of fear than to bask in the light of love. You need something bigger, stronger, and more overwhelming to displace your fear, and that's what love is. The bigger the love, the more completely it washes away fear. "There is no fear in love, but perfect love casts out fear, because fear has to do with punishment. Whoever fears is not perfect in love" (1 John 4:18). If you want to get rid of fear, go where love is.

Going where love is starts with being around loving people. You have a choice about who you spend time with. Think about who in your world lifts you up, encourages the best in you, helps you want to be a better person, and stimulates your growth. Seek out opportunities to be around those people. Perhaps that's a group of fishing buddies, a few girlfriends who meet up for coffee, or a specific support group.

It may feel unnatural to accept love from other people. You may need to make a conscious choice to let people love you and to believe what they say to you. Even the most sensitive and valuable gift won't do you any good unless you choose to accept it. If your spouse is loving, you may need to make the same choice to accept the love he or she has to give you.

If you want to get rid of fear, go where love is.

The most extravagant and undiluted love comes from God Himself. Love is God's very nature; it's who He is. "God is love" (1 John 4:8). You've heard that perhaps for years, but you may have never let that reality permeate your soul and wash out everything that's not consistent with that truth. Your head believes it, but you need to let that truth take an eighteen-inch journey downward—from your head to your heart. When your heart knows it, accepts it, and lives it, then your fear will drain away. The effect of God's love on fear is like the effect of light on darkness; the fear just can't stay.

Ask yourself, "How would I live today if I truly believed that God is love? How would I treat the people around me? What risks might I be willing to take? What selfish indulgences might I be able to let go of? How would my character begin to change? What obstacles would suddenly appear unimportant?"

God's love is not simply a warm fuzzy feeling, although He does have those feelings toward us. His love includes the care of a shepherd, the tenderness of a mother, the guidance and discipline and provision of a father, the fierceness and jealousy of a lover, the pride and trust of a master, and the rejoicing of a redeemer (Ps. 23; 103:13; Hos. 2:14; Zeph. 3:17; Matt. 25:21; James 5:11). He knows the glory for which you were created, and He has dedicated Himself and all the resources of heaven to see that you can be with Him forever and experience all that glory.

How do you come to know that kind of love? Spend time in God's presence. Letting God's love go from your head to your heart takes time. Ask Him to show His love to you. Invite Him to go through the tough stuff with you; that will increase your ability to trust Him. Look up Bible verses about God's love, and spend time thinking about them. The more you come to know God's love not only intellectually but also experientially, the more fear will leave.

Keep your eyes on the future.

A huge part of fear is not knowing what's going to happen next. You imagine the worst, and that feeds your fear. When the outcome is certain, you're much better able to handle things, even if the outcome is poor. But you can handle just about anything along the way when you have a guarantee that the final result will be worth it.

That's what knowing Jesus is all about for the believer. Yes, Jesus promised us trouble here, but He also promised glory hereafter. And if His promise of trouble has come true, it only increases our confidence that the glory He promised will also come true. Paul was certain of this: "I consider that the sufferings of this present time are not worthy to be compared with the glory which shall be revealed to us" (Rom. 8:18). If you—when you—look back on your pain, fear, and trouble from the vantage point of eternity, you will say, "I wouldn't have wanted God to do it any other way. All that trouble doesn't even mean anything now. This truly is more than worth it."

Keeping your eyes on that future is something big enough, strong enough, and overwhelming enough to drown out your fear, even the fear of death. When the faith heroes of Hebrews 11 looked to that future glory, it mattered not whether they were delivered or tortured, alive or dead. The certainty of the prize at the end would be worth anything. (See Hebrews 11:33–40). And for those who are alive near the end of the age—that means us—against whom the devil unleashes his especially vicious attacks, being unmoved by the fear of death becomes one of our most powerful weapons against him (Rev. 12:11). We'll talk more about having no fear as a spiritual weapon in the chapters ahead.

You really can come to the place where in Christ you can say, "No fear here!"

HAVE NO FEAR

Fear is a natural human response that you, I, and many others have had to face. Though God understands our fear, He repeatedly directs us to not be afraid. The examples of Peter and others demonstrate the transformation that God desires to take us through, from being fearful to fearless.

Understanding the greatness of the God who wants to be with us helps us respond to Him with awe and worship. That's what the Bible means by "the fear of the Lord." Truly understanding who God is can encourage you and overwhelm your fear of anyone or anything lesser.

Three biblical steps to overcoming fear include learning and then taking action, allowing God's overwhelming love to move from your head to your heart, and focusing on the certain glory that God has promised in the future.

QUESTIONS FOR CONTEMPLATION AND DISCUSSION

1. Where have you allowed fear to control some aspect of your life? What do you think God is saying to you about your fear?

2. Describe your picture of God. What do you really believe about Him, not just with your head but with your heart?

3. What does love mean to you? How can the love of other people affect your fear? How can God's love affect your fear?

CHAPTER 9

HOW JESUS DEALT WITH EVIL

FROM THE MOMENT Jesus showed up on the earth, He faced opposition. The majority of people may not have understood Him or His mission very well, but Satan did—at least to some degree. Jesus's whole purpose in coming as a man was to save humanity, and that could not be accomplished without defeating and destroying the devil and his kingdom of darkness. The incarnation was, along with all its other aspects, an invasion into enemy territory.

For Satan and his realm, Jesus's presence here was an ultimate declaration: "This means war!"

Yet Jesus seemed completely unruffled by such strong opposition. He never showed fear or anxiety when He encountered demons or those controlled by them, or even Satan himself. We never see Him on a hunt for demonic activity; His focus on being about His Father's business of saving humanity seemed unshakable. But whenever Satan or his demons showed up, Jesus responded with absolute authority over them.

As difficult as our lives may seem, and as much demonic opposition as we may feel we are facing, we will never see Satan and his whole kingdom of darkness arrayed against us to the degree that Jesus experienced. We can learn a great deal by examining the ways in which Jesus dealt with evil while here. Your own fear and anxiety will lessen as you more fully appreciate Christ's authority over evil and what His victory means for you and me today.

When it comes to spiritual warfare, Jesus is our divine example, our suffering Savior, and our victorious King. Each of those dimensions is important. Some discussions of spiritual warfare focus on only one or two of those dimensions, but without them all our Christian life will be ineffective and distorted. So come along as we explore this freeing and invigorating look at the life of Jesus.

JESUS AS OUR DIVINE EXAMPLE

Perhaps my favorite summary of Jesus's life is that proclaimed by Peter when he described "how God anointed Jesus of Nazareth with the Holy Spirit and with power, who went about doing good and healing all who were oppressed by the devil, for God was with Him" (Acts 10:38). Everything Jesus did during His life and ministry was undoing what Satan had been doing. He was all about healing disease, setting people free from oppression, and saving them from sin. It's no surprise that the kingdom of darkness was threatened.

Jesus frequently encountered those who were under the control of demons. The Gospels make several summary statements about Jesus healing those who were possessed or tormented. (Examples include Matthew 4:24; 8:16; Mark 1:32–34; and Luke 4:41.) We have many stories of individuals set free in Jesus's presence and by His word. He healed the sick woman who "Satan has bound these eighteen years" on the Sabbath (Luke 13:16). He set free the epileptic boy brought by his father for healing when His disciples could not (Mark 9:25–27). He delivered the demon-possessed man who had been relegated to living in the tombs (Luke 8:26–40). Jesus always comes across as calm and composed, while the demons respond with desperate cries and fear of torment.

The people who witnessed Jesus cast out these demons were astonished. "They were all amazed, so that they questioned among themselves, saying, 'What is this? What new teaching is this? With authority He commands even the unclean spirits, and they obey him'" (Mark 1:27). Jesus knew He had authority over the demons, and He exercised it simply by speaking a command.

This was so very different from what those around Jesus were used to. Ancient Jewish literature recounts how the people of Jesus's day lived in certain fear of demons. The Dead Sea Scrolls contain a number of prayers and liturgies that were used to try to bring relief from demonic oppression. And Josephus describes an elaborate ritual involving roots and incantations and spells by which one Jewish exorcist Eleazar attempted to cast out demons.[1] Both the people in general and those who attempted to get rid of demons approached the whole idea with a great deal of fear and anxiety.

And here comes Jesus; He has no incantations, no spells, no rituals, no stylized prayers, no angst, no fear, and He doesn't get all worked up. Sometimes the casting out of demons became dramatic only because of their resistance to Jesus's words. The Gospel passages that summarize Jesus's actions make most such encounters seem almost commonplace and likely no more dramatic than a simple "Get out!" (Mark 1:34). No wonder the people were astonished!

The authority in Jesus's words

Every time Jesus encountered Satan or his demons, He responded with calm, authoritative words. This began at His initial encounter with Satan in the wilderness just after His baptism. Satan tempted Jesus to turn stones into bread, to cast Himself down from the pinnacle of the temple, and to bow down and worship him. Each time Jesus defeated him not with a display of power, but with His words.

But they are not just any words; they are words from the Old Testament Scriptures. "He answered, 'It is written: "Man shall not live by bread alone, but by every word that proceeds out of the mouth of God."'...Jesus said to him, "It is also written, 'You shall not tempt the Lord your God.'"...Jesus said to him, "Get away from here, Satan! For it is written, 'You shall worship the Lord your God, and Him only shall you serve'"" (Matt. 4:4, 7, 10).

Every time after this that Jesus encountered evil in His ministry, He responded the same way. He spoke with authority, and the demons had to leave. If the demons were causing any sickness or disease, it had to leave along with them. The Roman centurion understood this: "Lord, I am not worthy that You should come under my roof. But speak the word only, and my servant will be healed" (Matt. 8:8).

Keep in mind as you contemplate Jesus's words that this was not some magic show. God spoke the worlds into existence with His word. Jesus is called the eternal Word of God (John 1:1). The power and authority of God Himself was present in those words Jesus spoke. That's why He spoke as He did to Satan in the wilderness. God's power is present in His Word—in Scripture, as Jesus spoke it, and as you and I speak it as well.

Jesus exercised authority over Satan through expressing God's Word from Scripture. You will need to know God's Word in order to exercise authority over the enemy as well.

You can do it too!

Can you imagine the awed excitement with which Jesus's disciples heard Him say, "You want to do the same things you've seen Me do? You want to preach the good news, heal people, cast our demons, and raise the dead? Yes, you can! It's time for you to go out and do it" (See Matthew 10:8.) I can picture them going out two by two, perhaps wondering if it would really work. John says to Peter, "Did you hear Him say what I heard Him say? Do you really think we can do it?" And Peter responds, "You bet! And I'm going to the very first chance I get!"

On their way to the first village Peter, John, and the others would have rehearsed over and over again exactly what they had seen Jesus do and how He had done it. They would have remembered the words He used, the look on His face, and even the feeling in His voice. They would have determined to do it exactly as their master had done. The results were spectacular! They must have had a predetermined time and meeting place to catch up with Jesus again. When they got there they exclaimed,

"Lord, even the demons are subject to us through Your name" (Luke 10:17). They would have acted as Jesus did, with no fear, no rituals, no anxiety, no long stylized prayers. They just spoke in Jesus's name.

So what does this mean for you and me? What does Jesus as our divine example show us about dealing with evil?

- Have no fear or anxiety. We have absolutely no need to experience fear or anxiety in our encounters with Satan or his kingdom of darkness. We don't go out looking for "a devil behind every bush"; there will be opportunity enough to exercise the authority Jesus has given us when evil presents itself. We are to be alert and firm, but not anxious. (See 1 Peter 5:8.)

- Fill your mind and heart with God's Word. If Jesus needed Scripture to successfully resist temptation and Satan, you will need it too. Spend time reading, studying, and memorizing the Bible. If those words are in your heart, the Holy Spirit will bring them back to your mind when you need them as you encounter evil.

- Remain focused on what God gives you to do. Jesus and His disciples remained focused on ministering to the hearts, minds, and bodies of people. The fact that doing so aroused Satan's opposition was almost secondary. Remain focused on what God has given you to do, and neither more nor less. If accomplishing that mission stirs up the devil's opposition, so be it.

Maintaining your focus is important. C. S. Lewis wisely opined that thinking too much or too little about Satan and his kind are equally dangerous traps: "There are two equal and opposite errors into which our race can fall about the devils. One is to disbelieve in their existence. The other is to believe, and to feel an excessive and unhealthy interest in them. They themselves are equally pleased by both errors."[2] My own research demonstrates the same thing. I studied a group of people attending a nondenominational church conference and compared their spiritual practices with their psychological well-being. Those who thought most frequently about Satan and demons causing them problems were much more likely to suffer from anxiety, depression, and generalized psychological distress.[3] It's your focus that's important.

Thinking about the devil too much or too little—
neither is healthy psychologically or spiritually.

Jesus encountered evil more than any of us ever will, and He expected His followers to face the kingdom of darkness in the same way He did.

JESUS AS OUR SUFFERING SAVIOR

We have talked earlier about how the war between the kingdom of God and the kingdom of darkness is not about power or territory. Jesus did not win His victory against Satan through a show of force, but through sacrificial love. We cannot expect to share in His glory without also sharing in His suffering. Paul said, "I want to know Christ—yes, to know the power of his resurrection *and participation in his sufferings*, becoming like him in his death" (Phil. 3:10, NIV).

Any human analogy of our salvation is incomplete, but imagine you and I are held hostage by a vicious enemy who has legitimate power to steal, kill, and destroy. Jesus saves us not by coming in as if leading a raid by Special Forces, killing our captors in the process. If He had done so, our sin would have killed us—eternally. Instead, our salvation is more like an exchange of hostages in which Jesus takes our place. On the cross He experienced the full force of Satan's power, and we are set free.

Some discussions of spiritual warfare leave out the enormity of sin. The reality is that you and I are in trouble—much deeper trouble than we usually imagine. Adam and Eve's fall brought sin into every aspect of our world and our character. The image of God in which we were created is obscured by our inherited sinful nature (Ps. 51:5). We grow up in and live in a sinful environment where evil happens to us and around us. Decisions made by others cause us harm and elicit sinful responses on our part through our attempts to simply survive. Our own sinful choices add to our brokenness and separate us further from God.

If we awaken even a little bit to our sorry state, Satan is only too quick to step in again. Self-righteousness seems a pleasing alternative: We're not really all that bad, are we? Or Satan may suffocate us with shame and guilt—some of it real and some of it false. And if we respond out of either self-righteousness or shame and guilt whenever we attempt to take a stand against him, we are certain to be defeated.

That's why, before we engage in any other spiritual warfare, we must humble ourselves before God (1 Pet. 5:6). We are completely hopeless and helpless on our own. As Martin Luther expressed it, "Did we in our own strength confide, our striving would be losing."[4] Trying to use our own natural or spiritual force against Satan is a sure pathway to further brokenness and despair. Remember, Jesus did not win against Satan by force, and neither can we.

Dealing with guilt

If you've been a Christian very long, you've probably experienced the attack of guilt. You are just starting to feel as though you're making spiritual progress, gaining victory, and making a positive impact for the kingdom of God, when some sin or weakness from your past or present hits you in the face. "Who do you think you are? You have no right or ability to move forward. Your sin disqualifies you, and you might as well give up!" It may sound as if your own head is saying those words, but it's the accuser of the brethren up to his dirty tricks again. (See Revelation 12:10.)

And he's right as far as he goes. Your human nature is sinful. You have sinned. It's certainly possible that you are sinning now.

But praise be to God, Jesus the suffering Savior has dealt with that problem already. He became sin for you, that you could become the righteousness of God in Him (2 Cor. 5:21). Jesus's suffering was real. His body was broken, His soul tormented, and His blood spilled for your redemption. He took your sin so that you can be free, and He offers you forgiveness for your past and transformation for your future.

Sin makes us vulnerable to Satan's attacks. Sometimes it's our own sin, and sometimes it's someone else's. Jesus is the only One who voluntarily made Himself vulnerable though He was sinless. "For the ruler of this world is coming, and he has nothing in Me" (John 14:30, NKJV). Once we choose Jesus as our Savior, we can come to the place where he has no hooks in us either.

You're reading this book because you don't want to live with fear and anxiety. You want freedom, victory, and joy. Guilt is one of the surest ways to keep you from experiencing that freedom. Ask yourself if you know Jesus as your suffering Savior. Have you allowed Him to wash you clean from everything in your past? Have you humbly and gratefully accepted the forgiveness He offers you? Have you determined to continue to allow Him to transform you into the person He needs you to be? If the answer is yes, rejoice in the freedom He brings. If the answer is no, what are you waiting for?

There's nothing in the Bible about needing to be perfect or mature before you can experience Christ's victory. The more you grow, the more victory you can experience, but even new Christians can live in freedom. The point is that you're clean—not perfectly clean in the ultimate sense, but clean in the washed, forgiven, and submitted-to-Christ sense. You're not going up against the enemy with your own righteousness, and you're not living in shame and guilt. You've agreed with God about what He says about you, that you're a new creation in Christ (2 Cor.

5:17). You remain humble before God and increasingly grateful for the unspeakable gift of Jesus.

Suffering as the way to victory

At the end of His ministry Jesus fully understood that His impending suffering and death were at the instigation of His archenemy and that His death would accomplish Satan's defeat. "Now judgment is upon this world. Now the ruler of this world will be cast out" (John 12:31). And Paul proclaimed the same thing: "Having disarmed authorities and powers, He made a show of them openly, triumphing over them by the cross" (Col. 2:15). It was through Jesus's suffering that Satan was defeated.

Victory is a result of suffering? The cross is the pathway to triumph? We've become psychologically jaded to how upside-down that was to the kingdom of darkness, and how scandalous that is to the human way of thinking both then and now. This truth is one of the great paradoxes of the kingdom of God.

What does Jesus as our suffering Savior mean for you and me?

- Sin is serious. Jesus dealt with sin on the cross. And you and I will have to deal with sin if we are to experience victory over fear and anxiety or over any other oppression from the enemy. The way to deal with sin is through accepting Christ's forgiveness for our past and His transforming grace for our future.

- Our suffering is to be expected. We don't anticipate it, but we expect it. Suffering is part of our experience as followers of Jesus. Jesus's acts of deliverance and healing while on the earth did not eliminate all suffering then or now. It's right to work to relieve suffering in our own lives and that of others, but we shouldn't be surprised when suffering still remains.

- Suffering precedes glory. Suffering is not an end
  in itself. Jesus rose again in triumph after His
  suffering and death. God can turn our suffering
  around for His glory. Some of that glory we can
  experience in this life—through knowing Him
  more deeply and becoming more useful for His
  kingdom. Some of that glory we will experience
  only when Jesus returns.

JESUS AS OUR VICTORIOUS KING

If the incarnation was an invasion into enemy territory and a declaration of war, then the cross was the declaration of victory. The rule and reign of God was established in truth on the earth, and Satan and his kingdom were defeated. The kingdom of God is here now, even while we wait for its complete realization at Jesus's return. Jesus declared this while here on the earth. The early church recognized this reality, and we can live in this reality even while we await the ultimate victory in the end.

What Jesus said about victory

Those around Jesus struggled with the whole idea of king and kingdom while He was here. Jesus frequently talked about the kingdom of God. For at least some of the Jewish people, that idea signified victory over the Romans. We know from the Dead Sea Scrolls that at least some also understood that the kingdom of God meant right winning out over wrong, good ultimately triumphing over evil. Jesus's primary message was that the kingdom of God is here—now (Mark 1:15).

As Jesus was teaching, preaching, healing, and setting people free from Satan's oppression, He was increasingly criticized by the religious leaders. In one of His answers to their criticism Jesus replies, "But if I cast out demons by the Spirit of God, then the kingdom of God has come upon you" (Matt. 12:28). The fact that Jesus was healing and delivering people demonstrated that the kingdom of God had truly come. Gregory Boyd says it this way: "For Jesus, healings and exorcisms clearly did not merely symbolize the kingdom of God—they *were* the kingdom of God. They were not byproducts of the message he proclaimed—they were the message. Warring against Satan and building the kingdom of God are, for Jesus, one and the same activity."[5]

On the human front Jesus was killed because He was a king. What Pilate and the others did not fully understand was that He was not king over any earthly realm. But He was—and is—still King. "Jesus answered, 'My kingdom is not of this world. If My kingdom were of this world, then My servants would fight, that I would not be handed over to the Jews. But now My kingdom is not from here'" (John 18:36). Establishing the kingdom of God in reality on the earth was the whole reason for Jesus's presence here. And being a king means rulership, authority, dominion.

Before He returned to heaven after His resurrection, Jesus gave His disciples instructions that we call the Great Commission. Jesus begins by affirming His victory over all the power of the enemy. "All authority has been given to Me on heaven and on earth" (Matt. 28:18). That's why He can direct His followers to "Go therefore and make disciples of all nations" (Matt. 28:19). The word *authority* is significant. The Greek *exousia* that is used here signifies absolute power, having both the capability and the right to act.[6] Nothing is left outside of Jesus's authority. He has won victory over them all: Satan and his kingdom of darkness, sin, sickness, death, the natural realm, and the unseen realm.

When Jesus returns, it will be as King of kings and Lord of lords (Rev. 19:16). Satan and his demons will be eliminated; there will be no more tears or sorrow or suffering (Rev. 21:4). Death will be done away with. His victory will be complete and eternal.

God's kingdom on the earth

Knowing that Jesus has been victorious and will ultimately rule victorious sounds wonderful, but you're struggling with fear and anxiety now. You don't want to wait. Perhaps you've prayed and you're still not seeing results. You may have had other people pray for you or tried to fight spiritually, and you still aren't experiencing freedom. All this "kingdom of God" stuff is just a nice-sounding spiritual idea if it does nothing for your present circumstances.

Consider what the early followers of Jesus said and experienced. First and most important, the kingdom of God on the earth meant they could live in "righteousness and peace and joy in the Holy Spirit" (Rom. 14:17). Their internal reality was changed. Their soul could experience true freedom regardless of their external circumstances. They were not bound to the religious rituals, fear of the unknown, or slavery to sinful practices they had lived with previously. It was the ultimate experience of "you don't have to live this way any longer!"

That freedom was available to everyone—rich or poor, Jew or Gentile, man or woman, slave or free. It was real and free for the asking. You couldn't work hard for it. If you've ever experienced spiritual bondage and then experienced freedom through Christ, you know the exhilaration and joy that such freedom brings—your sins are gone, and you are free to live for Christ and to experience His transforming grace in your life through the Holy Spirit.

But the kingdom of God also meant trouble for the early believers. They experienced miraculous healings, but people still got sick. Some were raised from the dead, but others died. People shared their material goods with one another, but some still suffered from poverty. Their internal reality affected their outward reality in part. And more than that, their affirmation of the lordship of Jesus stirred up all kinds of opposition—both from earthly authorities and from the kingdom of darkness. Some were ostracized from society, misunderstood, persecuted, or even killed. In my study of church history I have been most amazed by how consistently opposition resulted in the spread of the kingdom of God.

During the time between the cross and Jesus's soon return the kingdom of darkness is defeated, but not yet eliminated. We can experience true freedom from bondage as a result of Jesus's victory, but complete freedom from trouble will come when God makes everything new. Our life, mind, body, family, ministry, and everything about us can—and almost certainly will—be attacked by cross fire as Satan displays his evil anger at God and His kingdom.

That cross fire is not a reason for fear and anxiety. It is, however, a reason to become wise and alert to the enemy's ways, to put on your spiritual armor, and to learn to protect and defend yourself and those God has put under your care.

Evil institutions and social justice

Our world has struggled under the weight of sin so long that in many ways evil has become institutionalized. It's been that way ever since the tower of Babel. (See Genesis 11:2–9). Some have taken the whole spiritual warfare idea and applied it largely to fighting for social justice. The early church certainly saw persecution from evil institutions that were staunchly opposed to Christians.

> The kingdom of darkness is defeated, but not yet eliminated. Living in the kingdom of God brings real victory, but not freedom from trouble now.

The list of "evil institutions" around today could be debated, but it certainly includes human trafficking, the pornography industry, slavery, racism, extreme poverty, ethnic cleansing, and more. Some would include corporate greed, pollution of the environment, the glorification of violence and sex in media, and many others.

Jesus as Lord of all certainly means He is Lord above all human institutions—religious and secular. It's dangerous, however, to confuse the gospel with social justice—or politics or education or environmentalism or anything else. "The kingdom of God is within you," Jesus stated (Luke 17:21). It's right to work for the betterment of our fellow human beings; in fact, God would ask nothing less of us. But the gospel is first and foremost about hearts—the allegiance of you and me and others to God—and following Him.

I believe Jesus would say to those who care about these social matters, "Work for social justice, but don't leave the matters of the heart undone. Keep your priorities correct." The kingdom of God means that the woman held as a domestic slave can be free in heart and mind regardless of her circumstances—even while we work to set her free. It means the illiterate child can know God's healing and presence even while struggling to learn to read. It means the minority believer can live with courage in the face of persecution or death—even while we seek to promote social justice and religious freedom.

Do we work for social justice? Yes! We must simply remember that doing so is a result of our understanding of the kingdom of God and not its first, primary, or ultimate goal.

The believer and demonic oppression

A question needs to be addressed here before we get into the strategies for spiritual warfare in the coming chapters: Can a believer be oppressed or possessed by Satan or his demons?

When God created you, He gave you command and control of your own mind. He created you "a little lower than the angels" (Ps. 8:5). If you're reading this, you have the capacity to decide who you will serve. If you've decided to serve the Lord, no one—not even Satan himself—can pluck you out of His hand (John 10:28–29). Unless you voluntarily choose to remove Jesus as Lord of your life, you are secure.

This does not mean, however, that the devil cannot have an effect on you. Living in freedom is a choice, but it may involve significant risk and struggle. If you're living as a slave to fear and anxiety, it may be that you have not yet begun to live in the full freedom with which Christ has set you free. The rest of this book will help you experience that freedom in practical ways.

Satan can harass you as a believer. He can throw darts at you. (See Ephesians 6:16.) But he cannot sit on the throne of your heart and possess you unless you choose for him to be there. This again is no reason to live in fear. Christ's victory against the kingdom of darkness is real, and it means you don't have to be a slave any longer!

Walking in Christ's victory

Living in freedom may take getting used to. God had a lot of work to do in turning the children of Israel from a nation of slaves (when they left Egypt) into a people ready to take the land of Canaan. When God set me free from my own "four years of hell," I had a great deal of growing up to do in order to live in freedom. The rest of this book is about you learning to live in the freedom Jesus's victory makes available to you.

Remember that learning strategies of spiritual warfare is not about the methods. Techniques that you simply wield on your own will never bring you the victory you seek. We've talked about it already; successful spiritual warfare begins with submitting to God and allowing Jesus to be your Savior and Lord. It means you cast everything you struggle with onto Him—your sin, your fear, your anxiety, your problems. It means you're committed to following Him, and in doing so to cooperate with Him for the good of His kingdom in your own life and in the world.

What does Jesus as our victorious King mean for you and me?

- God's kingdom begins now. Jesus's victory on the cross means He is Lord of everything—including our own lives if we let Him. His kingdom is primarily a matter of the heart. That means we can live in real freedom now regardless of our outward circumstances.

- Final victory is yet to come. The kingdom of darkness is defeated, but not yet eliminated. In the meantime we will experience trouble—in part from Satan and his kingdom. But the final outcome is absolutely certain. Satan, sin, and everything ugly and terrible, including sickness and death, will be done away with when God makes all things new.

- It's God's kingdom, not ours. Christ's victory and spiritual warfare are not for the purpose of making things the way we would like them or for our outward earthly success. We experience victory too, but precisely to the degree to which we remain aligned with what God is doing.

I'm excited that you want to experience more of Christ's victory. It's real, and it can be yours.

FACING EVIL

Jesus faced evil continually during His time on the earth. Whenever He was confronted with Satan or his demons, Jesus faced them with calmness and authority rather than fear and anxiety. He exercised that authority with His word, based on the Word of God.

Jesus is our divine example in the way in which we are to face evil and how we exercise authority over the kingdom of darkness. We too must move past fear, fill our minds with God's Word, and remain focused on the mission God has given us to fulfill.

Jesus is our suffering Savior as He gained victory over the kingdom of darkness through His death on the cross. Our sin and guilt make us vulnerable to the enemy, and accepting Christ's forgiveness for our past and transformation for our future brings us freedom. Suffering precedes glory.

Jesus is our victorious King in establishing the kingdom of God in reality on the earth and in assuring us of complete and final victory when God makes all things new. We can live in real victory over the kingdom of darkness now even as we await the full realization of the kingdom of God soon to come.

QUESTIONS FOR CONTEMPLATION AND DISCUSSION

1. How do the ways in which you have tried to face or deal with evil in your own life compare with Jesus's example while here on the earth?

2. Has guilt made you vulnerable to Satan's attacks? Are there places in your life where you need to experience and accept Christ's forgiveness and transformation?

3. In what areas of your life have you been unaware that you are a slave? Where do you most need to experience Christ's victory?

PART III

STRATEGIES OF SPIRITUAL WARFARE TO DEFEAT FEAR AND ANXIETY

Above all else, guard your heart, for everything you do flows from it.
—Proverbs 4:23, niv

Therefore submit yourselves to God. Resist the devil, and he will flee from you.
—James 4:7

Now the salvation and the power and the kingdom of our God and the authority of His Christ have come, for the accuser of our brothers, who accused them before our God day and night, has been cast down. They overcame him by the blood of the Lamb and by the word of their testimony, and they loved not their lives unto the death.
—Revelation 12:10–11

CHAPTER 10

STRATEGY ONE: GUARD YOUR HEART

Preventing the Devil's Entry and Recognizing His Attacks

O N September 11, 2001, four US planes were hijacked by al Qaeda terrorists, and within hours nearly three thousand people were dead. The United States, and in some respects the entire world, would never be the same again. It was a wake-up call as significant as Pearl Harbor, the 1941 attack that brought the United States into WWII.

How could this happen? The bipartisan 9/11 Commission spent nearly three years asking that question and concluded that although the attacks on 9/11 were a shock, they were not a surprise. In the executive summary of their report is this sobering statement: "The most important failure was one of imagination. We do not believe leaders understood the gravity of the threat."[1] There were adequate warning signs that could have alerted us in advance if only leaders had been paying attention.

You and I have an enemy that is wiser, stronger, and more determined than any al Qaeda terrorist. But "we are not ignorant of his devices" (2 Cor. 2:11). We have been given adequate warning and more than enough tools to detect his activity, protect ourselves, and move forward in our mission for the kingdom of God.

Again, there is a significant danger in discussing techniques of spiritual warfare. Doing the right thing must never be allowed to take the place of developing and maintaining a relationship with the right Person. This war is first and foremost about our allegiance. Strategies can only be truly effective when your heart is fixed on Jesus.

Will you make mistakes in this warfare? Of course. Will you be wounded in the fight? Almost certainly. Will you still face problems even if you do everything right? Absolutely. But along the way remember that Jesus's victory is real. His freedom, His presence, and His joy are available to you regardless of your outward circumstances or inward struggles. You can leave fear and anxiety behind as you walk in that victory.

The first strategy in spiritual warfare is to guard your heart. That means becoming alert to where you are vulnerable, recognizing when you are under attack, and taking the necessary steps to protect yourself.

THINGS THAT MAKE YOU VULNERABLE

You lock your house and your car. You regularly change your passwords for critical online accounts. (You do that, right?) You make sure your children have their vaccinations and take their vitamins. These measures don't guarantee hackers or thieves or disease won't affect you and your family, but these precautions are smart.

> Doing the right thing must never be allowed to take the place of developing and maintaining a relationship with the right Person.

It's the same way with the kingdom of darkness. We know many of the ways in which Satan attempts to steal, kill, and destroy. Your heart is more precious than anything else you possess, and it's worth extraordinary effort to guard it well. "Above all else, guard your heart, for everything you do flows from it" (Prov. 4:23, NIV). Think of it as putting double locks on the door to your home or highly encrypted passwords on your computer. You are in charge of what gets in and what stays in.

Here are several filters to put in place to guard your heart.

Paying attention to these filters could mean the difference between life and death in your spiritual warfare.

Eliminate evil in any form.

This is the most obvious filter to have in place. Playing around with the occult is like giving a predator the key to your house; you're just asking for trouble. This includes demonic symbols or rituals; Ouija boards, tarot cards, or similar artifacts; attempts to communicate with the demonic realm or use demonic power for your own purposes; or visiting psychics or other individuals who claim to have supernatural insight or knowledge that does not come from God.

Guarding your heart is like putting a lock on your door or encrypted passwords on your computer. It makes you less vulnerable to the enemy's attacks.

The power or knowledge obtained from these sources may seem—or be—real. Satan can see and do *some* things that we cannot. He cannot foretell the future in the way God can, but he's often better than human beings at interpreting current events and human actions and using them to predict what is likely to happen in the future. In many respects he can manipulate events and people who are uncommitted to Christ to his liking. He's had thousands of years to study human behavior, and he uses that knowledge to wreak havoc. Satan does have a certain power in this world; don't be fooled into thinking that everything supernatural comes from God.

Be suspicious also of anything that comes from a non-Christian worldview. That would include New Age spirituality, Eastern religions, secret societies, humanism, Reiki, and energy healing. This category also contains yoga, acupuncture, and hypnotism. Perhaps the bristles on your neck are starting to rise as you read this. Don't these practices do good for people? From outward appearances, perhaps sometimes yes, but that's not the point.

Certain activities or practices may do some good things but may still make you vulnerable to the enemy's attacks. Remember, you're putting an encrypted password on the door to your heart!

Further, be alert to the values promoted by the seemingly innocent media you allow into your mind. Ungodly values around sexuality and gender issues, violence, money, marriage, and other issues are present everywhere. The specific song, Internet site, magazine, or TV program may not be especially evil in and of itself, but if the values it promotes are ungodly, you lower your defenses by allowing it into your mind. It makes you more vulnerable to the kingdom of darkness.

So what criteria should you use when deciding what to allow in? It's a deeper question than whether or not something is overtly "Christian." Here are three questions to consider:

- What is the source?

- What is the result?

- Can you, in prayer, picture Jesus engaging in that activity with you?

Especially if you struggle with fear and anxiety, I encourage you to be suspicious of anything mentioned! If the source is a worldview inconsistent with Christianity, be suspicious. If the result leads you away from the kingdom of God, be suspicious. If you feel a question in your heart about some activity, place, or person, spend some time in prayer about it. Consciously choose to put your own wishes aside and hear what God has to say. Study the Bible without looking to justify what you want. If after honestly taking your question before the Lord you still have any hesitation, eliminate that thing from your life. It would be much better to miss out on something you desire—even if it's good— than to put your peace and your eternal destiny in jeopardy. If you're wrong, God can let you know that in the future.

Finally, what if your work or ministry involves seeing evil? Law enforcement, security personnel, health care personnel, social service workers, pastors, teachers, missionaries (both here and abroad), and many others see evil in its worst forms. You may even face the issue in your own home as a parent or perhaps a spouse. First, make sure your own heart is clean. Take extra precautions to keep your soul filled with the good things of God. Second, continually pray for God's protection over your own heart, mind, home, family, and ministry. You are not invincible in your own strength. If you come to the place where you are being influenced by the evil around you more than you are influencing them, get away. Even Jesus and His disciples needed time alone away from the crowds.

Eliminate bitterness and unforgiveness.

Holding on to a grudge may feel so sweet, but doing so opens a door to the enemy. Paul encouraged forgiveness as soon as possible "lest Satan should take advantage of us" (2 Cor. 2:11). In the parable of the servant who refused to forgive his coworker a small debt after his master had forgiven him an enormous debt Jesus concluded, "His master was angry and delivered him to the jailers until he should pay all his debt. 'So also My heavenly Father will do to each of you, if from your heart you do not forgive your brother for his trespasses'" (Matt. 18:33–35). Refusing to forgive is more than just a bad idea. These Scriptures teach that persistently refusing to forgive makes us vulnerable to attacks from Satan.

Forgiving is good for your health. Refusing to forgive has been tied to a number of adverse psychological and physical health outcomes such as poor sleep, high blood pressure, and coronary heart disease.[2] Placing conditions on whether or not you will forgive has been tied to increased mortality.[3] Learning to forgive significantly decreased symptoms of anxiety (including PTSD) and depression among women who were struggling to restart their lives after leaving an abusive relationship.[4]

Many people find forgiving to be difficult. It may help to understand what forgiveness is not as much as what forgiveness is. Forgiveness is not saying everything is OK. It's not excusing someone's behavior or denying the hurt that resulted. Forgiveness is not a feeling, and it does not always result in restoration of the relationship. You can forgive whether or not the other person accepts your forgiveness or is even still alive.

Forgiveness is choosing to give up your right to seek revenge and leaving that up to God. Forgiveness is refusing to allow that person's behavior to continue to hurt you in the present. Forgiveness is setting yourself free and choosing to move forward into your future. Forgiveness is responding as Jesus would. Forgiveness is difficult, it's personal, and it's a process.

Corrie ten Boom struggled with forgiveness herself after being imprisoned and tortured by the Nazis during World War II. In the years after the war she often spoke about forgiveness and maintained rehabilitation centers to help others find healing from the atrocities of the war. But not everyone recovered: "Those who were able to forgive their former enemies were able also to return to the outside world and rebuild their lives, no matter what the physical scars. Those who nursed their bitterness remained invalids. It was as simple and as horrible as that."[5]

You can continue to drink the poison of bitterness and hope someone else dies as a result, or you can choose to do the difficult work of forgiveness. I wish for you the freedom of forgiveness!

The shadow of your past

So you have a past. Who doesn't? If having a past characterized by failure, abuse, sin, family dysfunction, addiction, violence, or any other baggage was enough to exclude you from Christ's victory, then Abraham, Moses, David, Peter, Paul, and all the other friends of God we read about in the Bible would also be excluded. And so would everyone who has been used by God in the two-thousand-year history of the Christian church. If God waited to find people without a past before using them, He'd have nobody to work with!

So what do you do with your past? You face it, turn it over to God, and get over it. Each one of those three steps is important. You can't move past something you don't address honestly and completely. There *are* things in your past that make you vulnerable to Satan's attacks. Look at both what happened to you and what you may have done with open eyes. It may be a family history characterized by violence, addiction, dysfunction, occult involvement, or habitual sin. It may be your own substance abuse, sexual behavior outside of marriage, flirting with evil, or some other mind-set or behavior that is outside of God's best. Ask the Holy Spirit to show you what hooks the devil may possibly have in you.

Second, turn all those aspects of your past over to God. Jesus died on the cross to make it possible for you to start fresh. Nothing is too big for Him to forgive. Agree with God about your past—regardless of who was at fault or how small or large the brokenness. Give Him access to every corner of your heart. Choose to accept Jesus's sacrifice on the cross as enough for you. Ask Him to examine you, cleanse you, and then fill you with Himself. (See Psalm 51:7; 139:23–24; John 14:23.)

Third, God doesn't expect you to stay stuck in self-examination forever. He has work for you to do. Once you have thoroughly dealt with your past, move forward. "Brothers, I do not count myself to have attained, but this one thing I do, forgetting those things which are behind and reaching forward to those things which are ahead, I press toward the goal to the prize of the high calling of God in Christ Jesus" (Phil. 3:13–14). Once you are clean, the devil has no hold on you. As the saying goes, when he reminds you of your past, remind him of his future. It's time to focus on the mission God has given you to do; don't be distracted.

It is possible to try to move forward too quickly. If you haven't completely dealt with your past, you won't be able to truly move forward, or you'll do so only with a ball-and-chain pulling you backward. Abuse, sickness, addiction, dysfunctional family circumstances, divorce, grief from the death of a loved one—have you truly examined your past and let God cleanse, heal, and transform you? If you're not sure, spend some time considering that question. Then you'll be able to move forward in victory.

People who draw you away from God

People are not the enemy, but sometimes people can be used by the enemy to distract, disturb, or torment you. It's possible to fall into the trap of thinking someone you dislike is an agent of the enemy. That's usually not the case. There are, however, some people whose effect on you is to draw you away from God. Spending time with those people can make you vulnerable to Satan and his kingdom.

Jesus loved—and loves—everyone, but He didn't like everyone the same. While on the earth He didn't offer His time and energy indiscriminately. He focused most on those who could and wanted to learn from Him (His disciples), those who needed and wanted His help (the sick or oppressed), and those who could support and encourage Him (such as Mary, Martha, and Lazarus). You can and should focus the majority of your time, energy, and resources on the same kinds of people.

When Nehemiah was leading the Jews in rebuilding the wall of Jerusalem after they had returned from Babylon, some in the surrounding countryside set out to thwart and destroy their efforts. Nehemiah refused to stop and talk with them: "I am doing a great work, so I am not able to come down. Why should the work cease while I leave it and come down to you?" (Neh. 6:3). If he had left his work, he would have put himself in great danger.

Jesus Himself, shortly before His final trip to Jerusalem, had to rebuke Peter when he tried to dissuade Him from following the path His Father had laid out for Him. "Get behind me, Satan! You are an offense to Me, for you are not mindful of the things that are of God, but those that are of men" (Matt. 16:23). Jesus recognized Satan's influence on Peter because of the attempt to get Him to change course from what God wanted Him to do.

The kind of people who make you vulnerable to Satan's attacks are those who would influence you away from what God wants you to do. The kind of people to avoid are those who would draw you into sin or those who would distract you from your mission by busyness, negativity, fear, or confusion. They may or may not be bad people, but regardless you need to stay away.

Protect your heart from these vulnerabilities with the same dil-igence you would protect your priceless jewels from a determined thief or your child from a known predator. Watch out, and the kingdom of darkness will not be able to harass you as easily.

KNOW WHEN YOU ARE UNDER ATTACK

Guarding your heart and life from Satan's attacks is critical, but it is just as important to recognize his attacks on your mind when they do come. Like alerts from an identity theft protection ser-vice, recognizing the characteristics of his attacks can allow you to resist them and get on with your life. It's part of being aware of the enemy's plans against you.

Satan can certainly use external things to oppose what God is doing in and through you. But much more insidious—and often much more effective—are the internal pressures he brings. I do not believe Satan can implant thoughts directly into a believer's mind, but he is a great pretender who can whisper in words that sound like our own voice. It is incredibly easy for most of us to quickly buy into his messages as if they were our own thoughts. That's why we need to be aware of the differences between his messages and those that come from God.

Jesus said, "The thief does not come, except to steal and kill and destroy. I came that they may have life, and that they may have it more abundantly" (John 10:10). So if there is stealing, killing, and destroying going on, we can know that it is the thief at work. Here are some warning signs that may show up in your own mind that can alert you to when the enemy is at work.

Confusion is not from God.

During what I call my "four years of hell"—my struggle with fear and anxiety—confusion was one of the primary things going on in my mind. I was a young physician looking good on the outside. Inside, however, I was tormented with a level of pain that made me wonder how long I could survive. Some of that was the result of a very dysfunctional upbringing. I sought help from various professionals and carried various diagnoses, but I still spent hours literally curled up in tears or hours walking in an attempt to find relief.

That was many years ago; people who have known me in the years since then have a hard time believing me when I tell them how dysfunctional I was. I had always believed God had the answer, but my torment began to end when I moved from knowing about God to knowing Jesus personally. I learned how to apply the various principles in this book to my own mind and heart, and I learned what it means to walk in Christ's victory. One of the most important things I learned was that confusion is never from God. When confusion is present, it's always a sign that the enemy is at work.

Several Scriptures make this clear. Paul wrote, "God is not the author of confusion, but of peace" (1 Cor. 14:33). It's the enemy who blinds, darkens, and messes with minds (2 Cor. 4:4). Instead, "God has not given us a spirit of fear, but of power and of love and of a sound mind" (2 Tim. 1:7, NKJV). If you feel confused, the source of whatever you're feeling, thinking, or wrestling with is not God, but the kingdom of darkness. The Holy Spirit may stir up your mind in order to correct some wrong attitude or behavior or to press you forward in your mission for God, but He will never cause a cloud of confusion and darkness in your mind. If that's what you're feeling, it's Satan's work, not God's.

What's the answer? Just stop! Quit trying to figure things out when your mind is filled with confusion. Put up a mental stop sign. Don't keep on playing into the enemy's hand and accepting the confusion he is trying to bring. Quite literally stop thinking! Distract yourself if need be. Deliberately put your mind somewhere else. Ideally that somewhere else would be somewhere peaceful such as nature, calming music, worshipping God, or listening prayer.

Later, when your mind is clearer and calmer, you can return to the issue. Don't worry that you will miss God; He will not shout His voice into the cacophony of sounds in your head. He is very patient, and He'll wait until you're calm and able to hear

His voice. He is well able to make Himself known to you when your mind is ready to listen: "Be still, and know that I am God" (Ps. 46:10). When you are ready, listen for His voice.

You may need to repeat the routine over and over until it becomes a habit and the enemy knows he can no longer use confusion to get to you. And any time in the future when you feel that tension of confusion rising inside your head, you can do it again.

> When faced with confusion:
> - *Stop!* Quit trying to think or figure things out.
> - *Calm* yourself. Put your mind in a place of peace.
> - *Listen.* God's voice will become clear when your own mind becomes quiet.

Condemnation is not from God.

Oh, don't you love the verse, "There is therefore now no condemnation for those who are in Christ Jesus" (Rom. 8:1)? We are set free!

And yet the Holy Spirit is not finished with us yet. We have growing up to do. Parts of our character need to be changed. The Holy Spirit is the One who convicts us when we sin and need to be corrected.

It's important to understand the difference between condemnation, which is always from the enemy, and conviction, which comes from the Holy Spirit. Condemnation always draws you downward. It's hopeless and dark and holds you in the past. It feels like the end. Conviction, on the other hand, draws you upward. There is hope, light, and a focus on your future. The Spirit's conviction points the way to receiving God's forgiveness and provides strength to go forward. It feels like the beginning. Condemnation and conviction couldn't feel more different, and the results couldn't be more opposite.

If you are feeling condemned in your heart, you can know—with absolute certainty—that it is not from God. "For God did not send His Son into the world to condemn the world, but that the world through Him might be saved (John 3:17). Go back to Scripture. Read John 3:16: "For God so loved the world that He gave His only begotten Son, that whoever believes in Him should not perish, but have eternal life." Read John 6:37: "He who comes to Me I will never cast out." Read Luke 19:10: "For the Son of Man came to seek and to save that which was lost." Choose to believe that you are exactly the one for whom Jesus came and died.

Condemnation from the enemy feels hopeless, dark, and holds you to your past. Conviction from the Holy Spirit brings hope and light and points you to your future.

If you are feeling conviction from the Holy Spirit, you will know what to do. "If we confess our sins, He is faithful and just to forgive us our sins and cleanse us from all unrighteousness" (1 John 1:9). Ask for God's forgiveness. Make things right with others to the degree it is within your power to do so, and then get on with the mission God has given you to do!

Control and manipulation are not from God.

We need guidance, encouragement, teaching, protection, and sometimes even correction. There are levels of authority in business, society, government, the church, and even in the home. Our institutions, all the way from the family to entire nations, need authority in order to maintain peace and allow human beings to thrive. Our well-being is often affected by how well those in authority fulfill their responsibilities. Paul said Christians should honor these authorities: "Render to all what is due them: taxes to whom taxes are due, respect to whom respect is due, fear to whom fear is due, and honor to whom honor is due" (Rom. 13:7).

But Satan has a sinister way of twisting God's concept of authority and turning it into manipulation and control. In the home this has resulted in domestic violence and the subjection of (usually) women and children to the whims and desires of (usually) men. In the church this has resulted in toxic religion, cults, twisted applications of church discipline, and attempts at "elder" control of minute aspects of people's lives. People trying to control you may say that it's for your own good, but when another human being attempts to control or manipulate you for their own purposes, you can be sure it is Satan's work and not God's.

Jesus came as a servant, and those who rightly exercise His authority will do the same. "He who is greatest among you shall be your servant" (Matt. 23:11). As I mentioned earlier, Jesus never delegated to any human being the right to play junior Holy Spirit in anyone else's life. If someone is trying to play that role in your life, be very suspicious. They may or may not be doing it intentionally, but if manipulation and control are in play, you can be certain it's not from God.

Countering Satan's attacks on your mind

If you sense confusion, condemnation, or control and manipulation going on in your mind, you know it's from Satan, whether or not it's directly from him in the moment, or more generally as a result of our sinful fallen world. Fear is a common emotion when these attacks are going on. Use these feelings as a barometer to alert you that something is wrong, but do not use them as a true test of reality.

Be especially cautious about making any decisions out of these feelings. You will almost certainly regret any decision you make that is based on fear, confusion, or condemnation. Use your precious emotional energy to calm your mind and enter God's presence. Use the techniques discussed in coming chapters, such as using the power of your words and entering into worship. Wait for God's clear answer before reacting in ways you'll later wish you had not.

By becoming alert to the characteristics of the enemy's attacks, you will be much better able to resist them and to counter them with what God has to say.

PROTECT YOURSELF

Guarding your heart with determination is like putting a double lock on the door to your home or encrypted passwords on your computer. It puts a filter on what you allow inside and prevents Satan from gaining free entrance into your life.

Eliminate evil in any form from your home and your life. Learn to do the hard work of forgiveness so that bitterness will not make you vulnerable. You and God together deal with your past so you can become free from its baggage. Stay away from people who would keep you from doing what you know God wants you to do.

Understanding the characteristics of Satan's attacks on your mind will make you much more able to resist him. Be alert for confusion, condemnation, and control and manipulation. These are never from God. Counter them with the truth of what God says and by entering into His presence. Seek God's answer for your circumstances, rather than trying to figure it out on your own.

Pray this prayer as you seek to implement strategy one in your stand against the enemy:

> *Dear Lord, I am weak and vulnerable in my own strength. You have won complete victory over Satan and the kingdom of darkness, and I need Your victory in my life now. I confess and renounce everything in my life that is not of You or that makes me vulnerable to the enemy's attacks. I turn away from everything evil in my past or in my present, and I ask You to wash me clean. I accept Your forgiveness for my own sins, and I ask for Your help to forgive those who have wronged me. Please walk with me through everything in my past that holds me in bondage, and guide me as I learn to walk forward in freedom. I ask You to show me the people in my life whom I need to stay away from and whom I need to learn from or minister to.*

Lord, my mind can be vulnerable to Satan's attacks, and I ask for Your power and discernment to recognize them when they come. You are not a God of confusion, condemnation, or control. Forgive me for attributing those attributes to You. Help me to quickly recognize the characteristics of the enemy's work. I choose to accept the sound mind You have promised me. I choose to listen to the Holy Spirit's conviction when I need to change. I choose to submit to You as the ultimate authority, and to the other authorities You have allowed in my life, but not to any control that comes from the enemy. I ask for Your grace and protection as I continue to learn to walk in the victory You have made available to me.

Amen.

QUESTIONS FOR CONTEMPLATION AND DISCUSSION

1. What is an area of your life where you may have allowed the enemy entrance without realizing it?

2. Describe a time when you felt confusion, condemnation, or control/manipulation in your mind. Looking back, can you recognize how that was the work of the enemy?

3. Describe something you can do when your mind seems overwhelmed by such an attack, such as call a friend, get alone with God, or listen to calming music.

CHAPTER 11

STRATEGY TWO: STAY CONNECTED

Locking Arms With Fellow Warriors

THERE ARE GOOD reasons why personnel such as police officers, paramedics, and others who are likely to encounter dangerous situations normally work with a partner. *Rambo* may have made money as a movie, but one soldier does not make for an effective army. Even Jesus longed for and sought out support from His closest friends when He was facing the biggest battles of His earthly life. You and I need others in our corner fighting the same battle alongside us.

Nurturing healthy connections with others may come naturally to you. If so, be grateful. Or perhaps you struggle with an ongoing case of independence, as I do. Although we value other people, some of us feel most at ease when we're alone—even when we are lonely. It takes conscious effort for us to determine who should be in our lives and what we need to do to remain connected. Let me assure you that especially when it comes to spiritual warfare, the benefits of leaving your lone ranger modus operandi behind are well worth it.

If you struggle with fear and anxiety, developing and growing connections with others may seem even more difficult. People can and probably have hurt you. It's normal to not want to be hurt again. Locking the doors of your soul feels safer even when it's lonely inside, but you can't keep your doors permanently locked and be free at the same time. It may feel risky to venture out, but it's absolutely necessary if you want to overcome fear and anxiety.

The Bible talks about how important it is to be connected:

> Two are better than one, because there is a good reward for their labor together. For if they fall, then one will help up his companion. But woe to him who is alone when he falls and has no one to help him up. Also if two lie down together, then they will keep warm; but how can one keep warm by himself? And if someone might overpower another by himself, two together can withstand him. A threefold cord is not quickly broken.
>
> —Ecclesiastes 4:9–12

Let's look at what healthy godly connections with fellow warriors look like, what others can and can't do for you, and steps you can take to nurture the right kinds of connections.

DISCERNING HEALTHY CONNECTIONS WITH OTHERS

It may seem almost a contradiction to talk about nurturing strong connections with others when we talk about spiritual warfare. In the previous chapter we talked about avoiding people who would draw you away from God. Much of what you have experienced as the enemy's attacks may have come through other people. Worrying about what other people think may be one of your biggest anxiety struggles. Toxic religion in your past may have left you fearful of trying church again.

That's why it's important to look carefully at the kinds of people you connect with and the types of connections with them that you nurture. Human connections are absolutely vital to your well-being as a whole and to your victory in Christ in particular, but it's not connecting with just anyone. Jesus was intentional about the kinds of people He invested Himself with, and you should be too.

What kinds of people to invest with

Other people in your life will generally fall into one of three categories. First, some people are clearly on your side. As a believer that should be synonymous with being on God's side. Sometimes this is clear—your walk with God is strengthened when you are with them, your heart is encouraged and filled, and you leave encounters stronger in spiritual battles than you were before. When you find people like this, be willing to invest a lot of yourself in order to nurture these connections. You are blessed indeed if you have a few such fellow warriors in your inner circle to journey with.

Second, there are people whose heart may be on God's side but their effect on you is less clear. They may seem abrasive or make you feel uncomfortable. Some may make your life diffi-cult or wear you out. You may not understand each other. Jesus's disciples were often in this category, and yet He invested a great deal in them. The point is not how comfortable you are together; the point is their heart as best as you can know it. You may not open your heart to these people as much as to your inner circle, but you need them in your life.

We said earlier that Jesus spent most of His time and energy on three kinds of people: those who wanted to and could learn from Him, those who needed and could receive His help, and those who could encourage and support Him. If someone is on God's side and you can either learn from them or they can poten-tially learn from you or receive your help, they have a place in your life.

Another way to think of the same principle is that you need people who are ahead of you, with you, and behind you on this journey. You need people in your life who are a little further along than you are, who have experienced victory in the very kind of battles you are facing and can provide some inspiration and guidance. These may be spiritual or life mentors, professional helpers, etc. You also need people in your life who are peers, who see the world in similar ways as you do and are facing the same type of struggles as you are. You lock arms with these people as fellow soldiers in support and encouragement. Last, you need people in your life who you can give something to. You may not feel as though you have much of anything to give, but there is always someone behind you on the journey to whom you can say, "I've been there, and I found the way forward. Let me help you find the next step."

The third category of people in your life are those who are neither clearly on your side nor clearly evil. They may or may not have an effect on your daily life. Your attitude toward these people should be twofold. First, don't spend too much energy worrying about them. A lot of energy is wasted in worrying about what "they" will think or do. And second, whatever mission God has given you to do will involve them in some way. Your purpose is always bigger than yourself. At some point God will send you to a certain group of them. Learn to see them as Jesus sees them. Be someone whose character becomes attractive to them, and become alert to the appointments God makes for you to draw them into His kingdom.

And then there are those who are clearly not on God's side. Some people are truly used for evil in your life. When faced with these people, remember, we are not fighting against flesh and blood (Eph. 6:12). The kingdom of darkness may use people to oppose God's work, but our spiritual warfare is not against human beings. I have heard Christians say in so many words to someone who disagrees with them, "I am against you, says the Lord." That is an abuse of Scripture. Spiritual warfare is to be used against Satan and his demons. Be excessively cautious before moving against other human beings. We can judge behavior, but only God truly knows the heart.

Jesus rebuked and cast out demons who were harassing people, but He didn't confront human beings in the same way. He spoke truth and engaged with people, but He also never allowed them to deter Him from His own position or mission. For you, when you encounter evil people, protect yourself—both physically and spiritually if necessary. Then stay focused on what God has given *you* to do.

Toxic religion

Not every person or institution that carries a Christian label is on God's side. As you make efforts to connect with fellow soldiers in spiritual warfare, you also need to be aware of those who may look or sound godly on the outside, but who are waiting to infect your spiritual hard drive with malicious viruses that will destroy your effectiveness and peace. Perhaps you've already been seriously wounded by toxic religion and wonder if all churches are similar.

Church can be messy. Any time human beings are involved, there will be problems. The group of Jesus's closest friends, His disciples, had problems. But God hasn't changed His plan to build His church, regardless of how people—or the enemy—try to distort it. Here are a few spiritual viruses and issues to watch out for in your own spiritual journey and in the group of fellow warriors you connect with:

- Rigid perfectionism. God sets a high standard. The problem is when we focus primarily on a rigid list of external behaviors more than on the heart change that God requires. This often results in people being mean-spirited and angry, and their own efforts to live right often break down and some secret sin becomes exposed. The better alternative is to focus on God's grace and on allowing right behavior to result from His transforming work in people's hearts.

- Cheap grace. Jesus offers us grace—complete, free, unending, and undeserved. There's nothing you have done, or can do, that can make God love you either more or less. But His grace does not stop with your past; He loves you enough to offer—and require—your transformation. (See Romans 6:15.) Cheap grace stops half way through. The true gospel combines both complete forgiveness for your past and a pathway of hope toward your complete transformation going forward.

- Playing junior Holy Spirit. No human being can or should play God in your life. One of the ways God speaks to you is through people, but that should never take the place of hearing His voice for yourself. If leaders or fellow believers use God talk to manipulate and control you, be very suspicious. Don't allow any human being to have the place in your life that only God should occupy.

If religious people are displaying the characteristics of the thief—stealing, killing, and destroying—it is not from God (John 10:10). If confusion, condemnation, and control are the primary characteristics of the religious people you're around, it's time to make a change. Healing from toxic religion can be painful and take a lot of time. Know that God does have healing available for you, and He will help you find healthier connections with other fellow warriors.

WHAT OTHERS CAN AND CANNOT DO FOR YOU

Going it alone is a bad idea. But now that you've come to understand the kinds of people you need in your life, what can you expect them to do for you? Some people regularly complain that their life is miserable because those around them—their family, their pastor, their boss, their friends—aren't doing what they are supposed to. Approaching life with such an entitlement mentality will always result in disappointment. On the other hand some people struggle to accept any help from anyone, perhaps because that would mean acknowledging that they can't do it all for themselves. If you struggle with either of these approaches to people, you need to discover anew some things about healthy relationships.

Let's look at what you can reasonably expect to get from your connections with others and what you cannot expect. If you find yourself disappointed in people, you may need to search out other friends. But perhaps even more, you may need to adjust your expectations.

What others cannot do for you

First, other people cannot fight your battles for you. If your version of spiritual warfare is primarily asking others to pray for you, you have a lot of growing to do. Having others pray for you is critical, but you need to be doing your own fighting. What that looks like will vary during different seasons of your spiritual life, and sometimes you will have greater or lesser amounts of strength to fight for yourself. You must see yourself as a warrior. That may look like learning all you can about lifestyle, right thinking, and prayer. It may mean doing the hard work of learning to live free of an addiction or learning how to forgive. It may mean practicing the strategies in this book that you haven't done before. The point is that you must be active in the process. You lock arms with others to fight alongside one another; you don't ask them to do your fighting for you.

Second, others cannot fix you or fill you up. You must learn to feed your soul nourishing food, just as you do your body. Food may include things such as insight, perspective, intimacy, peace, stimulation, rest, refreshment, discipline, love, beauty, joy, and more. You're responsible for finding what fills you up and doing what it takes to get more of that. It doesn't matter how wonderful your spouse, your pastor, your best friend, your therapist, or your small group buddies are. They cannot make you whole. You don't create the soul food, but you must choose to take into your soul what you need. In addition to time with people, that may mean spending time in nature, listening to music, reading Scripture, and being in solitude. There is also an extremely important sense in which only God can fix you and fill you up. Don't look to other people to do what only God can do for you.

Lock arms with others in order to fight together.
Don't ask them to fight your battles for you.

What others can do for you

What do soldiers, police officers, or others in dangerous situations look for from their buddies or partners? Those are some of the same things you can expect from fellow warriors in your spiritual battles. Here are some of them:

- Warnings of danger. Your pastor or a fellow believer may see or sense a spiritual danger that you aren't sensitive to. That doesn't mean you don't protect yourself or that you accept what someone else says without thought and prayer, but you may save yourself a lot of trouble by listening to warnings from others who have a different or larger perspective.

- Encouragement. Going through tough stuff becomes easier when someone is there to go through it with you. You're not the only one struggling: you know that "the same afflictions are experienced by your brotherhood throughout the world" (1 Pet. 5:9). You mutually help each other to keep going and not give up. You remind each other of the end of the story, where Jesus wins.

- Bringing in God's presence. Jesus promised that "where two or three are assembled in My name, there am I in their midst" (Matt. 18:20). It's easier to doubt God's presence when you're battling alone. And when believers come together in His name, God's presence shows up in an extra dimension. Prayer, worship, praise—all that and more are often sweeter when they are done together.

- Greater effectiveness. Whether it's a health battle, character growth, relationship challenge, or learning new thinking, you will make much more progress when you do it with someone else. It's more than encouragement; other factors come into play, factors such as accountability, practical help, and a broader perspective. You will experience greater success by allowing others to join you on your journey of growth.

- The opportunity to give. You become stronger when you have others counting on you. Focusing outside yourself takes your mind off your own problems and brings out the best in you. Connecting with people helps you develop strengths you never knew you had and provides motivation to continue to grow.

On the fear and anxiety front, Dr. Kenneth Pargament has studied what factors in spirituality are correlated with better (or worse) psychological well-being. Seeking connection with others in a community of faith was a significant part of what he calls a "positive religious coping pattern" that led to fewer symptoms of psychological distress and greater positive spiritual growth even when facing significant life stresses.[1] There is a whole body of scientific evidence showing that, in general, those who are regularly connected with a healthy community of faith tend to experience better physical, psychological, and spiritual well-being.

Professional help when needed

Fear and anxiety can make you feel very small. It may seem that reaching out to others will take more emotional energy than you have right now. If you're at that very difficult place, let me suggest that reaching out for help is one of the best ways to use the energy you do have. God has blessed His people with a lot of resources. Asking for help is not a sign of weakness; you have recognized how much you're in need, and you're taking a step toward getting better. If you're feeling stuck, it's time to get some help.

If any of these statements describes you, it's a good time to ask for professional help:

- You are frequently unable to think clearly because of your confusion, anxiety, or fear.

- You have tried to move forward on your own, but are making no progress.

- Your fear or anxiety are preventing you from functioning normally in your daily activities.

- You feel overwhelmed by taking any small steps to overcome your fear and anxiety.

If you haven't already, begin by getting a medical evaluation for any physical problems that may be affecting you. Then seek out a professional, a small group, or both where you can find some help for your psychological distress. A pastor who is experienced in such problems or a Christian counselor may provide you with support, perspective, prayer, and tools you need to move forward. A support group may also be enormously helpful. Consider a group that includes others struggling with your specific problem, or look for a Celebrate Recovery group in your area.[2] A support group may also help you connect with fellow warriors who can continue the journey with you long after your current struggles are improved.

I believe there is a place for medication and professional psychological therapy if you are not otherwise coping well. Needing such treatment does not mean you're a failure as a Christian or that you're weak. Think of it as doing what it takes to stay alive and begin to function while you are learning to experience Christ's healing and freedom. It's both/and; medical help and professional therapy if necessary along with prayer and spiritual warfare. God is still your healer and deliverer. If He uses human beings or medication to help get you through tough stuff, that's fine.

Professional therapy or medication when needed may be a means to help you stay alive and begin to function while you are learning to walk in Christ's victory.

HOW TO MAKE AND NURTURE CONNECTIONS
WITH FELLOW WARRIORS

There are some practical steps to find and develop connections with believers who will strengthen and support you in spiritual warfare. If your connections are strong already, simply review these thoughts for anything that can make your connections even more effective. If you struggle to make and nurture connections, these ideas will help you begin to do so.

Begin at church.

First of all, pray. Ask God to help you connect with those you need in your life. Ask Him to send the right people for you to connect with and to make you aware of them when they show up. There may already be such people in your life that you simply need to be aware of and reach out to.

If you are part of a community of faith, does your church seem reasonably healthy based on the points about toxic religion earlier in this chapter? Is the Bible taught and followed, and are people growing spiritually in your church? I believe God plants people in churches. Do you sense He has planted you there? If so, are you taking advantage of the growth opportunities already present? Are you actively seeking connections with other members? Ask your leaders for suggestions or join a small group already in place.

If you're not part of a community of faith now, at some point you'll need to take a risk and become part of a growing church. If the church you're in now is toxic, you may need to take a break, but only temporarily. Remember that you're not looking for perfect, but for a place where people are growing. Visit a few churches prayerfully. Take the initiative and talk to people there. Pray for God's clarity and peace in your mind when you find the place He wants to plant you.

Human relationships take time and effort to develop. One of the best ways to do so in church is to become part of a small group, such as a Bible study group that meets before services or during the week. It may also be a class or a growth or support group that meets regularly or a group organized around service or missions. Find out what groups are already meeting together at your church and join one. It may take many different forms, but you need to get close enough to a small group of fellow believers that you begin to do life together. When you begin to share life together with other believers, you begin to experience the benefits of connections in spiritual warfare.

How to use connections in spiritual warfare

You're facing a tough battle. Your fear and anxiety are churning, and you're struggling to keep your mind from following its usual self-defeating path. You recognize some of the characteristics of the enemy at work and you need some support from your spiritual warfare buddies. What does that look like?

Here are some practical tips for maximizing the benefits of your connections with other believers:

- Share your story. Even the most kindhearted family member or small group friend cannot read your mind. Sometimes the Holy Spirit will let another believer know that you need prayer, but don't wait for that. Find a safe place to share your story such as in your small group, with a godly mentor, or with a Christian counselor. You won't—and shouldn't—share all of your story with everyone. But don't hold back out of fear. The biblical principle is to "confess your faults to one another and pray for one another, that you may be healed" (James 5:16).

- Be open to receiving help. Let your heart be open enough to receive support back from those you share with. Ask for their perspective. Be willing to hear a different way of looking at your problem. Listen to what they have to say, but know you may hear some advice that's difficult to accept.

Check it yourself in prayer, but it may be the key
to moving forward.

- Ask for prayer. "Five of you shall chase a hundred, and a hundred of you shall put ten thousand
  to flight" (Lev. 26:8). Banding together in prayer
  is powerful. "If two of you agree on earth about
  anything they ask, it will be done for them by My
  Father who is in heaven" (Matt. 18:19). It's not
  that God doesn't hear you when you pray alone;
  He does! But joining together in prayer pushes
  back the forces of the enemy with greater effectiveness. Spiritual breakthroughs often happen
  as a result of a few committed believers praying
  together toward the same end.

- Offer your support in return. Receiving support
  and prayer from fellow believers is just the first
  part of the equation. You also need to offer your
  support and prayer for them in their struggles.
  That may not be at the very same moment that
  they pray for you, but remember how important
  it is to look outside yourself and find ways to give
  to others. That's part of the power of small committed groups of believers doing life together;
  they are there for you when you need it, and
  you're there for them as well.

If you've never experienced the benefits of other believers
praying for you when you face a spiritual battle, I encourage
you to take the risk and ask others to pray for you. That doesn't
replace your own prayers, but the power and encouragement you
will receive is more than you can describe in words. It's worth the
discomfort to take the chance and reach out.

FINDING COMMUNITY

You need at least three kinds of people in your life: those who are further along than you in their journey, peers who are facing similar spiritual battles as you, and those who are coming behind you. It's worth investing a lot in those kinds of relationships.

But not everyone is on your side or God's side. Protect yourself from those who may be evil. You may have been hurt in the past by toxic religion; give God permission to heal you and to connect you with healthier believers.

Establishing healthy connections with fellow believers happens best in a small group of some kind, where you can get close enough to begin to do life together. Then when any of you face spiritual battles, you can offer each other support, encouragement, and most of all spiritual warfare prayer that can powerfully push back the enemy.

Pray this prayer as you seek to implement strategy 2 in your stand against the enemy:

> *Dear Lord, please forgive me for trying to fight my battles alone and for isolating myself from those You have sent to help. I ask for Your wisdom and guidance as I seek out healthy connections with others who are also following You. I ask You to send the people I need into my life and to help me be aware of who they are when You send them. I ask for Your courage to move past my fear and anxiety as I seek to connect my life with others in Your body.*
>
> *I also ask for Your protection against those people through whom the enemy would seek to do me harm physically or spiritually. I ask for Your healing from the pain others have inflicted on me in Your name and in the name of religion, and that You lead me to the church where You want me to be planted.*
>
> *I accept Your plan for me to connect with other believers. Thank You for guiding me as I do so. Amen.*

QUESTIONS FOR CONTEMPLATION AND DISCUSSION

1. How good are you at connecting with other believers? Are you more prone to expect too much of them or to isolate yourself from others?

2. Have you been hurt by Christians displaying toxic religion? How has that affected your spiritual journey?

3. Name one thing you're going to do during the coming week to begin establishing healthy connections or to strengthen the connections you have.

CHAPTER 12

STRATEGY THREE: SPEAK UP!

How to Use Your Words in Spiritual Warfare

How wonderful it felt to be free from the spiritual bondage that had been tormenting me during my "four years of hell." I was learning about spiritual warfare, and I began pleading the blood of Jesus over my life every day. I knew there was no magic in the words themselves, but it was an awesome way to connect with Christ's victory regularly. My symptoms just didn't seem to be a problem any longer, and I was grateful.

Several months later I realized I was struggling again. The confusion and tears and misery started coming back. Hadn't Jesus set me free? I had a relationship with Him now, and wasn't I doing everything I knew to grow spiritually? The thought of deteriorating into my "hell" again terrified me.

I still remember the morning when it hit me. I was standing in the shower, praying and trying not to cry. I had begun to recognize the Holy Spirit's voice, and I heard it right then: "You stopped pleading the blood of Jesus. You're not protected." I had assumed that pleading the blood of Jesus was a short-term need, and now that I was "healed" it was no longer necessary. How wrong I was.

For the last twenty years or so I have continued to plead the blood of Jesus over my life—my spirit, soul, and body—out loud, every single day. It has become a regular part of life between me and God. My symptoms have never returned. I have never again felt the internal torment from which God had set me free. There are certainly other things that have been important in maintaining my spiritual freedom, including learning that I could choose to be happy, how to control my thoughts, and the other strategies I talk about in this book, but nothing in my life has been as consistently powerful as daily pleading the blood of Jesus.

If you haven't been around Christians who talk this way, this part of my story may sound very strange to you. I remember what a huge struggle it was initially for me to even speak the words "I plead the blood of Jesus." I knew Jesus died for me, and I knew He gained victory over Satan on the cross. But talking this way didn't make sense to me, and it may not make sense to you either.

I encourage you to keep reading with an open mind, prayerfully. Don't simply speak certain words because I suggest you do so or because you've heard others say them. There's nothing about magic or ritual here. Let God's Word and the Holy Spirit speak to your heart, and see what role your words need to have in your own journey of freedom through spiritual warfare.

WHAT WORDS DO IN SPIRITUAL WARFARE

Words are powerful. God spoke the universe into existence by His words. At least that's what Genesis 1 says. There is creative power in God's words. You and I are created in God's image, and our words have very real power as well—not in a magical sense or to the same degree as God's words—but what you speak does make a difference.

In Revelation John talks about God's final glorious victory over Satan and evil. It's an awesome picture:

> Then I heard a loud voice in heaven, saying: "Now the salvation and the power and the kingdom of our God and the authority of His Christ have come, for the accuser of our brothers, who accused them before our God day and night, has been cast down. They overcame

him by the blood of the Lamb and by the word of their
testimony, and they loved not their lives unto the death."
—Revelation 12:10–11

We'll look carefully at this scripture in this chapter and the next.

You are much more likely to both remember
and believe something you speak out loud
compared with something you simply think.

There may be plenty of accusing going on in your head if you're
struggling with anxiety and fear. Remember where that comes
from; it's not from God! And notice how God's people overcame
the enemy. "The word of their testimony" is a powerful weapon
against Satan and his kingdom of darkness. Your words affect
what happens both in the spirit realm and in your own mind.

Your words affect your own soul.

We've talked a lot about taking charge of your thinking, but
speaking words that support the outcome you are after is just as
important. Thoughts make a difference—a very important difference. But simply thinking something is not enough. Speaking
something brings it from inside your mind (as important as that
is) into reality.

When you speak something out loud, your brain engages
more parts of you than just your mind. Your mouth and throat
and lungs are physically engaged in forming the words. Your ears
hear the words that you say. Engaging the physical and auditory
parts of your brain creates a positive feedback loop; you're much
more likely to both remember and believe something you speak
out loud compared with something you simply think.[1]

But it's more than that. When you speak, aspects of your mind
and spirit are energized in ways that go beyond simply believing
and remembering. Emotions and deeper mental processes are
triggered. If your words are well chosen, parts of your heart can

OVERCOMING FEAR AND ANXIETY THROUGH SPIRITUAL WARFARE

be stirred up: you may have increased courage and hope, clearer thinking, and stronger faith. Your words become an actual means whereby the spiritual warfare in your mind is accomplished.

How do you choose the words to speak that will have such a positive impact on your own self? We'll get very specific later in this chapter.

Your words affect the spirit realm.

Jesus's authority while here on the earth rested first in His identity as God and His sinless life, but Jesus did not use any power while here that is not available to you and me. He exercised His authority through His words, such as when He rebuked sickness, stilled the storm on Galilee, or freed men and women from demonic oppression (Matt. 8:16; Luke 4:39; 8:24). Even the Roman centurion recognized that all Jesus had to do was speak and unseen powers had to obey (Matt. 8:8).

As a result of His victory over Satan through His death and resurrection, Jesus's authority over heaven and earth was forever established (Matt. 28:18). And He has delegated that authority to you and me as His followers. Jesus gave His disciples "authority over unclean spirits, to cast them out, and to heal all kinds of sickness and all kinds of disease" (Matt. 10:1). Peter, Paul, and the others in the early church took this seriously. And Jesus promised that all those who believe in Him would have access to the same authority (Mark 16:17).

Can you imagine Peter or Paul getting all upset or crafting some elaborate ritual when they encountered evil or were faced with someone controlled by Satan's power? Of course not. They simply acted as Jesus had, and in His name they commanded the demons to leave. And if you are acting as Jesus did, speaking in His name, the unseen forces in the kingdom of darkness must respond in the same way. This authority is delegated; it doesn't rest in the words you say or in your own force of character. Remember that in yourself you are no match for the enemy. You must be submitted to God first, and then His authority backs up the words you will speak as His representative.

Your words can also have another kind of effect in the spirit realm. If you speak in agreement with the "stealing, killing, and destroying" plans of the enemy, those plans will be strengthened. Your own mind hears the discouraging words, of course. Your words also align you with either God's kingdom or the kingdom of darkness. If you're agreeing with the enemy, it makes you more vulnerable to his attacks, increases his power in your life, and removes you from a measure of God's protection.

The power of words spoken to you

Even the words others speak to you, about you, or in your presence affect you. We all know the destruction that demeaning, critical, or abusive words can cause to your psyche, but there's more. If you mentally accept or agree with the negative, evil, or otherwise destructive words you hear, you increase their power over you.

The words you speak out loud align you with either the kingdom of God or the kingdom of darkness.

There were many times in your past, such as when you were a child, when you didn't have the understanding, maturity, or power to do anything but accept those destructive words. But now you're a believer in Jesus, and you're learning about spiritual warfare. You no longer have to blindly take in and accept what others say. The analogy is an old one, but it still fits very well: you may not be able to stop birds from flying over your head, but you can stop them from making a nest in your hair. You can choose whether or not to agree with what is said to you or about you, and you can either accept or reject the spiritual implications.

The enemy may use other people's words to mess with you. If you don't take into account the possible spiritual forces behind those words, you will naturally feel fear, anxiety, or other negative emotions. Not everyone who criticizes you is evil; some people are truly out to help. But watch for a red flag in your spirit when someone says something negative to or about you, or even when someone gives you a message that they say is from the Lord. Don't agree with them mentally or otherwise unless their words also agree with what you know of God, His Word, and His dealings with you individually.

If you sense that someone's words to you or in your presence are destructive to you, put a stop to them right then. You don't have to make a scene; if you're not in a position to say or do something to publicly stop them, you can resist the message mentally and remove yourself. I encourage you to also speak out loud your disagreement, even if it's soft enough for only your own ears to hear: "I do not accept the message those words would have me believe. I resist in Jesus's name, and I plead His blood over my mind and this entire situation."

WHAT DO YOU SAY?

Now for the practical part. If your words are powerful for spiritual warfare, what do you say? You just read a taste of this in the previous paragraph, and the rest of this chapter will give you several more specific examples of how to use your words. These are things you can begin doing right now, today, even as you read these pages. Pause and read aloud the words in italics; they're intended to be spoken out loud to help your mind, your mouth, and your ears begin to get used to this frontline weapon in spiritual warfare.

Here are five categories of fightin' words you need to speak as you move forward in experiencing Christ's victory for yourself.

Speak the truth.

That means the truth about everything: the truth about you, about your circumstances, about God, about His Word. Jesus said, "You shall know the truth, and the truth shall set you free" (John 8:32). Reading and studying the Bible is helpful in a large measure because it gives you concrete truth to both focus your mind on and to speak. Remember the Stockdale paradox we talked about? You must be brutally honest about what's going on right now and at the same time hold on to absolute faith in the outcome.

Some Christians have taught that acknowledging or verbalizing a problem is expressing a lack of faith. The Bible doesn't teach that. Read the Psalms; David and the other writers were free to verbalize their distress, weakness, sin, pain, anger, or any other problem to God. Verbalizing your problem to other believers is a way to find healing (James 5:16). Denying the truth about you and your circumstances by refusing to speak it only makes you more isolated from yourself, from others, and from God.

But there's more to truth than your human perception of the problems you are facing. Whether it's your own self-destructive behavior, sinful things that were said or done to you, or the onslaught of attacks from the enemy, living in this sinful world brings us pain. Looking as honestly as you can at the root causes of your fear and anxiety is part of speaking the truth. That may include speaking the truth about violence that was done to you in the past, a genetic heritage of anxiety, or lifestyle factors you have allowed that have led to increased distress.

But the truly ultimate truth is even greater still. "Jesus said to him, 'I am the way, the truth, and the life'" (John 14:6). Truth is a person—Jesus Christ. The more you come to know Him, the more Jesus—the ultimate truth—sets you free. The truth is that Jesus sees you, knows you, and cares about you. The truth is that He died to save you and redeem you in every area of your life. The truth is that He has invited you to live in His victory and to be an ambassador of His kingdom so others who don't yet know Him can also find freedom. The truth is that as bad—or as good—as this world gets, it's not the end. The truth is that we know the end of the story, and that is that Jesus wins!

Speaking truth—all of the truth, including what God says about the situation—does several things. It opens to God's transforming love the places in your soul where you may have been hiding. It helps your own mind remember and believe what God says about you and your problem. It breaks much of the power of fear and anxiety by helping your mind focus on God and on the future He has for you. It pushes back the confusion the enemy is trying to stir up. It puts the enemy on notice and aligns you with God's kingdom. And it invites the Holy Spirit into your situation.

Speak the truth out loud about you, your circumstances, God, and what God has done for you.

Here's what that may look like. Try inserting the truth about you and your own situation into these statements. These sentences are written as you speaking the truth to God. It's also a good idea to speak the truth to others—believers who can support you, a Christian counselor, or a pastor.

Dear God, I determine to speak the truth. Right now I'm a mess. I have done [anything you know you have done to contribute to your problem], *and it has caused me big problems. I am suffering from* [fear, anxiety, sickness, betrayal, or other consequences], *and I feel* [anger, hopelessness, fear] *because of this. So many things helped bring me to this point:* [family background, others' sins against you, etc.]. *It seems every other person and institution and the enemy himself is against me. I don't really know what to do next.*

But I know that You are truth that is much greater than what I see and feel about myself. You came and died and rose again for me, and You have overcome Satan and his kingdom of darkness. You have promised to cleanse me from my brokenness and sin, to transform me into Your likeness, and to give me Your victory. You have the solution to my problem. You have promised to give me everything I need and to be with me always. Nothing is impossible for You (Phil. 4:19, Matt. 19:26; 28:20). *Amen.*

Speak of God's greatness and goodness.

This is a continuation of speaking the truth. It's doing what David talked about: "Oh, magnify the LORD with me, and let us exalt His name together" (Ps. 34:3). When you magnify something, you perceive it as bigger. You're talking about the God of the universe; it's impossible to magnify Him too much. It's fine to tell God how big your problem is, and you should. But be sure to then tell your problem—and yourself—how big your God is.

"It Is No Secret" is an old gospel song that describes how what you have witnessed God do in others' lives, He can do for you as well. When Old Testament Bible writers were faced with problems, they would often begin rehearsing the great things God had done. Many of the psalms express this, such as Psalms 8, 18, 46, and 66. The whole story of Jesus is the ultimate demonstration of who God is and what He thinks about you and me. Much of the entire Bible is about how God deals with people and their problems—both in our lives right now and eternally.

There are at least three ways to fill your mind with God's goodness and greatness. First is, of course, the Bible. The second is to see or contemplate God's works in nature. Stand outside at night and look up at the stars; your God is bigger than all that. In fact, He made all that, and still He cares about you! I remember being overcome with amazement at God's creation when I was studying embryology—the astonishing way one single cell can develop into a human being. Take some time to really see God's works all around you. The third way is to listen to, read, or learn about how God has worked in other people's lives. You may hear such stories at church. Some Christian radio and TV programs tell such stories. You can read church history or stories about believers in the past who faced and overcame problems. It's not hard to find stories about how God helped people overcome addiction, sickness, trauma, fear, busyness, grief, or any other limitation or problem.

Once you have filled your mind with His goodness, speak it out loud. Doing so helps your mind grasp how good and great

God really is and drowns out the negative messages from the enemy. That might be something like this:

> *Dear Lord, You are greater than my problems. You spoke the world into existence with Your word. You keep the uncountable galaxies moving in space, with all their fiery suns and planets and untold wonders. Your power and greatness are displayed in the majesty of the mountains, the fury of the thunderstorm, and the vastness of the ocean. Your extravagant beauty and care for detail are displayed in the songs of the birds, the colors of the sunset, and the birth of the wild animals in the spring.*
>
> *And yet You care for us—the people You made in Your image. You brought Your people Israel out of Egypt and into the land of Canaan. You displayed Yourself in the miracles of Elijah and Elisha, the glory of Solomon's temple, and the prophets who foretold of the coming Messiah. You came in the person of Jesus, healing the sick and oppressed, walking the roads of Galilee with Your disciples, and dying for our sin—including mine. You rose again and ascended to heaven in glory, victorious over sin and Satan and death. Others have told of Your goodness and greatness throughout the centuries. And You are coming again to put an end to all sin and wrong. You truly are great—and good. Amen.*

Speak what God has done for you.

Not only is God great and good, and not only is Jesus the truth, but He has done great things for *you*. Don't ever forget those things. Hold on to them. Find a way to remember them; write them down in a journal, make notes in your Bible, collect small mementos, or in some other way make certain you record what He has done for you. It's one thing to recount what He has done for others; it's much more personal and impactful when you can speak of what He has done for you personally.

If you're reading this, He has done something in your life. If you haven't been recording those spiritual high points, think about it now. Think back to what your life was like before you came to know Jesus and how He made Himself known to you.

Think of how He changed your heart and brought you healing or peace or joy or life. Think of the times He has answered your prayer or shown you something of Himself. Think of the people He has placed in your life to bless you, and what you know of the purpose for which He put you on this earth.

Remember it, write it down or record it in some way, and then speak it out loud. When you are feeling down, go back, read, and remind yourself of these things. Tell others what God has done for you. "Then our mouth was filled with laughter, and our tongue with singing. Then they said among the nations, 'The Lord has done great things for them.' The Lord has done great things for us; we are glad" (Ps. 126:2–3).

Your story will be unique. That's part of the beauty of telling about God's work in your own life. These sentences are phrased as you talking to God, but it's great to speak this to others as well. Doing that might sound something like this:

> *Dear Lord, You have been so good to me. Even as I am now struggling greatly, I remember how You have always been there for me. I thought I was OK on my own, but You saw the true me. You showed Yourself to me when I was far away from You. You pulled my heart toward You and invited me to be Your own. You forgave my sin. You rescued me from a life of futility and showed me that You had a plan for me. Even when I haven't been listening very well, You have never left me alone. You have been patient with me and brought me the healing and deliverance that only You can.*
>
> [Insert your own story.] *You gave me the courage and the grace to keep going when my family had nothing for me. You kept me alive when I thought fear would overwhelm me. You brought helpers into my life just when I needed them. You showed me the gift You have placed inside me that You need me to share with others.*
>
> *What can I do but thank You? Amen.*

Plead the blood of Jesus.

Here we get into some nitty-gritty. Perhaps you've relaxed a little in the last few pages. Speaking truth, talking about God's greatness, and telling what He has done for you may seem tame enough, even if it might stretch you a little. But "plead the blood of Jesus"? That might sound weird.

Please don't check out now. All the speaking up to now has been absolutely essential. It has put you in a frame of mind to stay focused on Jesus. But warfare is bloody, and it's time to take the gloves off. The only way Jesus could gain victory over Satan and his kingdom was through shedding His blood and dying on the cross. Here's how Paul described it: "And having disarmed authorities and powers, He made a show of them openly, triumphing over them by the cross" (Col. 2:15). Without Jesus's shedding His blood for you and me, there would be no victory.

And we cannot experience victory in our lives now without His blood. It's not only a one-time thing two thousand years ago, or one moment when you first come to know Jesus. It's an every day, every moment thing. The enemy has not laid down his weapons, and until he is destroyed in the end, you and I will have to stay covered with the blood of Jesus. We will have to continue to live that way because we will never be strong enough to survive in our own strength. We will never be good enough to not need His cleansing from sin. We will never be able to claim victory apart from living in the victory that He achieved—through His blood.

The verse from Revelation makes it clear: "They overcame him by the blood of the Lamb" (Rev. 12:11). There is no other way to overcome Satan and his kingdom!

When Moses was about to lead the children of Israel out of Egypt, God instructed them to take the blood of a lamb and physically apply it to the door of their homes. That blood signified their membership in God's company and protected them from the destroying angel who came to kill every firstborn (Exod. 12:3–13). They were to remember that day forever in the Passover celebration as the time when God delivered them from their oppressors. It was also a foreshadowing of Jesus's suffering and death on the cross through which we would be delivered.

The Israelites would not be protected unless they applied the blood of the lamb to the door of their homes. And you and I cannot be protected unless we apply the blood of Jesus, the true Passover Lamb, to our lives. That's what pleading the blood of Jesus is all about. When you plead the blood of Jesus, it prevents the enemy from having the access to your life that he would otherwise have. Satan and his demons cannot stand when the blood of Jesus is applied; it shows them their defeat.

How do you do that? With your words. I encourage you to do this daily. I do. Specifically, out loud, place everything in your life under His blood. Plead His blood over any problem you have. You may also, as I sometimes do, prayerfully take your own private communion at the same time, physically taking into yourself the symbols of Jesus's broken body and spilled blood as you accept His sacrifice and victory for yourself. Here's what this may look like. (Remember, this is to be said out loud.)

> *I plead the blood of Jesus over my life right now—my spirit, my soul, my body. I plead the blood of Jesus over my spouse— spirit, soul, and body. And I plead the blood of Jesus over my children:* [name them individually]. *I plead the blood of Jesus over everything in my life that may be troubled; my fears, my anxiety, my sickness, my confusion, my brokenness, my sin, my anger, my worry about other people, my future, my job, my marriage, my money, my sex life, my eating, my time, my entertainment, my church affiliation, my thinking, my sleep. I place it all under the blood of Jesus, and I leave it there.*
>
> *I surround myself and my family today with the blood of Jesus. Let nothing affect me or my family that does not first come through the blood of Jesus—nothing from the enemy, from other people, or from the natural world. I let go of anything that cannot remain under the blood of Jesus— any habits, any material things, any thoughts, any people. I*

> *choose to remain under the blood of Jesus, and I claim His*
> *protection, provision, and direction today. Amen.*

Have you said those words out loud? Try it. These are the most important words to speak in your journey of spiritual warfare.

Speak to the enemy in Jesus's name.

You may sense in your own soul that a specific attack from Satan is a major factor in your distress. Some resources on spiritual warfare devote significant time and energy to laying out a hierarchy of demonology in the kingdom of darkness or describing specific evil spirits and their actions. Bible scholars don't generally agree on those specifics, and there's no evidence in the New Testament that Jesus spent much time worrying about them either. But there is abundant evidence that He gained victory over all the kingdom of darkness and has made that victory available to us. You don't have to study demonology in order to experience Christ's victory.

When Jesus encountered demons, He authoritatively told them to leave. He delegated to His followers the authority to cast out demons in His name (Matt. 10:1; Mark 16:17). Those in the early church took this seriously, and they continued to minister Christ's deliverance from demonic oppression (Acts 5:16; 8:7; 16:18). If you are a believer, you can do the same. Remember, Jesus didn't go around looking for a devil behind every bush, but when He encountered them, they had to obey His word. When you encounter them, they will have to do the same when you speak in Jesus's name.

If you sense a specific spirit oppressing you in some area, speak to it in Jesus's name, demanding that it leave your life. That may be a spirit of lust, spirit of adultery, spirit of greed, spirit of debt, spirit of perversion, spirit of sickness, spirit of fear, spirit of addiction, spirit of pornography, spirit of confusion, spirit of lethargy, or any other. It may be a spirit attacking your marriage, your children, your emotions, your finances, or your ministry. If you have a name or description that's fine, but don't get hung up on defining a name for the spirit.

Jesus told His disciples, "Whatever you bind on earth will be bound in heaven, and whatever you loose on earth will be loosed in heaven" (Matt. 18:18). Heaven will back you up when you speak in Jesus's name. However, this is not a carte blanche for exerting your own will over circumstances or people. Remember, your enemy is not your spouse, your boss, your friend, your coworker, or some human institution. Our warfare is against spiritual forces in the kingdom of darkness. That is the appropriate biblical application of binding and loosing.

Is there a demonic force oppressing your mind, body, life, marriage, family, business, or ministry? It's time to tell it to go. Here's what that may look like:

> *I speak to you, spirit of* [lust, greed, addiction, or whatever], *you spirit attacking my* [marriage, money, emotions, ministry, or whatever], *in the name of Jesus, and command you to leave now. I stand under the blood of Jesus. You have no right to my life, my mind, my family, or my marriage* [or anything such as my sex life, my money, my job, etc.]. *They belong to Jesus now and forever. In Jesus's name I command you to get your hands off what belongs to Jesus, to leave me, and to never return. I place the cross of Jesus between me and you, and you will not be able to penetrate the barrier of Jesus's blood and return to me.*
>
> *I affirm again that I belong to God the Father, His Son Jesus Christ, and His Holy Spirit. There is no room for you, evil spirit, in anything related to me. I bind you in Jesus's name from having anything to do with me or that which God has given me from now on. Go now, in Jesus's name, and do not return. I claim Christ's victory right now as my own, and I give the Holy Spirit full reign in my life and everything related to me. Amen.*

Continue to speak this way until you feel something strong arise in your soul. It's more than an intellectual disagreement;

it's a fierce resistance against Satan and his kingdom of darkness. Grab ahold of that sense of resistance in your soul, nurture it, and speak it out loud. Join with other believers, as discussed in the previous chapter, and ask them to pray this way with you. You can live in freedom, in Jesus's name!

FIGHTIN' WORDS

Words are powerful. Jesus expressed His authority over the kingdom of darkness with His words, and you can do the same in His name.

With your words, out loud, express the truth—about you, your circumstances, God, and His Word. Speak of His goodness and greatness, and what He has done for others and for you personally. Regularly plead the blood of Jesus over your own life and the lives of those you care about. And when you encounter demonic oppression or attacks against you, speak to the evil spirits attacking you to leave and return no more, in Jesus's name.

Go back and read, out loud, the italicized words in the last five sections of this chapter, speaking the words of spiritual warfare that align you with God's kingdom and free you from the attacks of the enemy.

QUESTIONS FOR CONTEMPLATION AND DISCUSSION

1. Can you think of words you said, or that were said to you, that have had a lasting effect on some aspect of your life? What do you think about the power of words?

2. What truth do you need to speak? Truth about you, or about God, or about what He has done for you? Speak that truth right now.

3. What happens in your mind when you try to plead the blood of Jesus or speak to the enemy to leave in Jesus's name? Is there some resistance on your part, or are you experiencing Christ's victory in this way?

CHAPTER 13

STRATEGY FOUR: HAVE NO FEAR

How Overcoming Fear (of Death) Defeats the Devil

Y OU MAY HAVE discovered the power of fearlessness while dealing with a playground bully, a business competitor, or some other rival. No opponent is more invincible than one who has absolutely nothing to fear. The most effective way to defeat your adversary is to exploit their fear—of exposure, of pain, of losing, of shame. One of Satan's most effective ways to defeat you is to exploit your fears. No one—not even the enemy—can hold anything over you if you come to the place where you are truly unafraid of the consequences.

Fear is a weapon Satan uses against us precisely because he knows that once we lose all fear, his attacks no longer have a place to land. You may have picked up this book because you're wrestling with fear and are hoping spiritual warfare will be a means to help you find freedom. And it will. Hopefully you're already experiencing that freedom as you've been working your way through these chapters. But freedom from fear is more than a benefit Christ's victory makes available to us; it is also one of the strongest weapons we have against Satan and the kingdom of darkness.

On February 15, 2015, we all saw images on the news of ISIS militants preparing to behead twenty-one Coptic Christians for the crime of believing in Jesus. This was just one more brutal incident in the long history of the persecution Christians have experienced in various cultures and parts of the world ever since Stephen was first martyred outside Jerusalem (Acts 7:59–60). We can't be certain of what was going on in the hearts of those twenty-one, orange-garbed, handcuffed Christians as they knelt in the sand, held by black-hooded terrorists, knowing their lives were about to end. But in the images we saw, their faces showed absolutely no fear.

After mentioning "the blood of the Lamb" and "the word of their testimony," Revelation says of those who overcame Satan that "they loved not their lives unto death" (Rev. 12:11). And the early Christian writer Tertullian observed, "The blood of the martyrs is the seed of the Church."[1]

You don't have to become a martyr to use freedom from fear as a weapon against the enemy. This is one of the ultimate ways in which God takes what the enemy meant for evil (your fear) and turns it completely around into a weapon by which you gain victory over him. (See Genesis 50:20.)

FEAR OF DEATH

Death and the fear of death has been one of the enemy's strongest weapons ever since sin entered this world. As a physician I see this regularly. Patients often make decisions about their health care out of their fear of death. It's not uncommon for patients to ask for tests or other procedures because they fear cancer or some other life-threatening condition, even if they have no physical symptoms that would indicate such. (Getting appropriate medical care is not the problem; we're talking about going beyond what is reasonable or medically wise.)

The fear of death reaches deeper than simply concern over the end of physical life. The Bible talks about the fear of death as bondage (Heb. 2:15). Death is the result of living in a sinful world. When a loved one dies or we face our own death, we are reminded how fallen and messed up everything around us is and how many things are out of our control. Just the thought of death stirs up thoughts—and fears—about what happens next.

The Bible paints broad pictures, but much about what happens after we die is still beyond our comprehension. We know enough from God's Word to make right decisions now, but there is still mystery and pain. Most of us would rather do just about anything else than think about our own death.

The topic of death has become much more personal to me recently. It has been less than three months since my husband died. The loneliness, sadness, and overwhelming grief still come in waves, and I know they will for a time. There's no way to make death OK. It's not supposed to be OK. God didn't create us to live a few years, or even many years, on this earth and then die. He created us to live forever. We were made for eternity!

But for those of us who believe in Jesus, death does not hold the same power over us as it does for others. The fear of death need not keep us bound. Jesus took on our nature "so that through death He might destroy him who has the power of death, that is, the devil, and deliver those who through fear of death were throughout their lives subject to bondage" (Heb. 2:14–15). Since Jesus died and rose again, we can know death is a defeated enemy and will eventually be completely destroyed. "The last enemy that will be destroyed is death" (1 Cor. 15:26). Jesus's resurrection proved that.

Death isn't supposed to be OK. God did not create us to live a few years, or even many years, on this earth and then die. He created us to live forever!

That's why those Coptic Christians could display no fear. That's why I personally can have hope even as I grieve my husband's death. That's why Paul really couldn't decide whether he would rather live or die:

> For to me, to continue living is Christ, and to die is gain. But if I am to live on in the flesh, this will mean fruitful labor to me. Yet I do not know what I shall

choose. I am in a difficult position between the two, having a desire to depart and to be with Christ, which is far better. Nevertheless, to remain in the flesh is more needful for your sake.

—PHILIPPIANS 1:21–24

When you lose the fear of death, Satan and death itself have no more hold on you.

What is greater than death?

Losing the fear of death does not mean you want to die or that you do not grieve when someone you care about dies. Death is not supposed to be pretty. Death is ongoing evidence that we still live in a world where the kingdom of darkness has power. But losing the fear of death does mean that something larger has grabbed your heart, something that is so great that death becomes relatively inconsequential by comparison.

When you were a child, there were things you were afraid of—perhaps the dark, monsters in the closet, a barking dog, or going someplace new. If you're a parent, you've had your child run into your arms when something frightened them, but in your presence monsters simply disappear. It's the same with you. Yes, death is that big bad monster in the closet that's out to get you. And it's even worse than that. The monsters your children feared were only in their imagination; death is only too real. It's final (in earthly terms), it's ugly, and it hurts—a lot. Remember, in the Bible death is a real enemy (1 Cor. 15:26).

But just like a parent whose loving arms can magically make monsters disappear, God's presence robs death of its power. Whether or not our lives on the earth continue, we know that this is not all there is. While we don't know all the details, we know enough about what happens next to know that we don't have to be afraid. Death is no longer an undefeated foe; death has been conquered. Because of Jesus we know that death is not the end of the story.

Seeing beyond earthly death disarms it of its power to terrify.

The rest of the story is that death will die, and those of us who trust in Jesus will live forever! The most famous of all scriptures—John 3:16—promises that those who believe in Jesus "shall not perish but have eternal life" (NIV). That life is eternal in two ways. First, it's never ending; death will be done away with, and we can never, ever die again. It's also eternal in quality. The best is yet to come! Human words cannot describe the overwhelming satisfaction and joy that will be our experience in heaven.

Remember Vice Admiral Stockdale in the Vietnamese POW camp? Having absolute faith in the eventual outcome does not remove our responsibility for living in reality here and now, nor does it prevent pain. But it does provide the fortitude and courage to endure and even to thrive through the absolute worst that the enemy can cook up. We have something to believe in that's much more reliable than Stockdale's faith in the United States armed forces. We have God's Word. We have proof of His Word in the resurrection of Jesus Christ. We know the end of the story!

Fearlessness as a weapon

There comes a time in an important conflict when you know you have won. The bully has tried his best to beat you up, and you haven't backed down. Your business competitor has put everything into trying to crowd you out, but you're the one with rising profits and market share. You come to realize that you've made it through the very worst that your adversary can throw at you, and you're still standing. In this fight you're invincible. You may still have challenges, but it's as good as over.

When you fully comprehend that you are on the winning side in this war between good and evil, that freedom from fear makes you invincible in the face of whatever the kingdom of darkness brings against you. It's one of the almost surprising but intensely satisfying benefits of spiritual warfare. You know that Satan has tried his best with you and he has lost. It's never going to get any worse than this, so you no longer have any reason to fear him.

That level of freedom only comes through intense warfare. It's not arrogance; it's simply a realization that you have won even though the battle is not yet over. There's a pervasive calmness, a fierce strength, and an unshakable faith that comes from that kind of victory. It doesn't result in lack of activity; there's still fighting to be done. But you know that you know that you know you are on the winning side. And for the Christian even death cannot shake that complete assurance of victory.

I believe that's the kind of victory those Coptic Christians and the other Christian martyrs experienced even at the moment of their earthly deaths. It's the kind of victory that allows me to carry on even after my husband's death. And it's the kind of victory you and I can experience regardless of what happens during the remainder of our lives here. It's not the kind of victory you go looking for, but when you successfully endure even in the face of the worst attacks of the enemy, nothing he can throw at you—even death—will be able to shake you.

If you're not at that place of victory yet, that's OK. The point is to not give up. If you're still struggling with fear and anxiety, don't give in. This may be the battle through which you gain that kind of victory. Like Vice Admiral Stockdale, you assess where you are honestly, and then you resolutely determine to maintain faith in your eventual victory. With God on your side, the outcome is assured.

And if you are in the middle of the fight of your life—literally or figuratively—know that there is a difference between calm faith and giving in. Faith is neither frantic nor lazy. You put all you have—no more and no less—into the fight, knowing that it's not enough in itself, but also knowing that you will win because of who your leader is. It doesn't matter if the battle takes your earthly life; that's a small price to pay for the glory that is to come.

HOW TO BECOME FEARLESS IN SPIRITUAL WARFARE

A child doesn't overcome their fear of monsters overnight (no pun intended). You as a parent disarm the power of the monsters by your presence, your child begins to experience success in overcoming their fear, and the fear gradually lessens until it no longer has any effect on them.

You will not overcome fear, including any fear of death, overnight either. It's something that develops as you continue to grow spiritually and as you experience increasing levels of freedom from fear. The point is to recognize that fear is from the enemy and to determine to never give up until it loses its hold on you.

Little battles prepare you for bigger battles.

A soldier is not dropped behind enemy lines the day he finishes basic training. Further training and preparation are essential before meeting the enemy face-to-face. The moment you said yes to Jesus, His victory became available to you, but it takes learning, practice, and experience to become able to confront the larger battles in spiritual warfare.

Little battles help you develop the courage, skills, and endurance you need to win the bigger battles. God said to Jeremiah, "If you have run with the footmen, and they have wearied you, then how can you contend with horses? And if in the land of peace in which you trusted, they wearied you, then how will you do in the thicket of the Jordan?" (Jer. 12:5). It may seem as though what you're facing right now is one of those bigger battles, and you don't have what it takes. But God has promised that He will not allow anything to come against you that is beyond your ability to endure and overcome. Whatever you're dealing with now is an opportunity to develop the habits, thought processes, prayer life, perspective, and character you need.

In order to learn from your present circumstances you must not accept defeat in the little things. Right now we're not talking about getting into heaven; that was settled when you accepted Jesus as your Lord and Savior. We are talking about becoming effective in spiritual warfare. If you have not yet learned how to deal with your emotions when things don't go your way at work, God will not put you in a larger position where increased stress or other people's actions would give you even more reason to lose your temper. If you have not yet learned how to take responsibility for what you can change and leave the things you can't change up to God, you won't be trusted with greater responsibilities where change will be even harder. If you have not yet learned how to move past your fear and anxiety when God asks you to take a small step of faith, you're not ready for an assignment that will arouse even more opposition and require more faith.

What are you up against right now? What little battles do you need to win today in order to gain strength for the larger ones that are coming? For me right now that means sitting down to write this book even when my emotions are struggling with grief. For you it might mean making a doctor's appointment to investigate any physical reasons for your anxiety even though it frightens you to do so. It might mean working the next step in your recovery from an addiction, making a loving statement about your faith when you know your friends or family will react negatively, or taking a step in a new direction you are certain God is leading you toward.

Joyce Meyer is known for her aphorism, "Do it afraid!" The more you act without letting your fearful feelings dictate your behavior, the more fear will lose its power. Don't wait to feel ready before taking an action step. Be thoughtful, ask for God's guidance, and then move forward—even if you're afraid. You don't win any battles by letting the enemy roll all over you. Your action may be asking for help, praying fiercely, taking responsibility for your role in the situation, or making a difficult decision. Whatever it is, do it!

Overcoming fear of death

Since fear of death is the biggest fear Satan uses against us, overcoming that fear is one of the tools we must develop in our journey of spiritual warfare.

Risks don't scare you when the outcome is absolutely guaranteed. When you know for certain what will happen, you don't get sidetracked as easily by problems along the way. A solar eclipse or a thunderstorm does not shake your faith in the sun coming out tomorrow. We have something even more certain than the sunrise to place our faith in when it comes to death, and that is the certainty of Jesus's victory over sin and death and our own victory over the same if we choose Him.

When I returned home from the hospital the morning my husband died, I sat down with a cup of coffee and my Bible. I opened it to 1 Corinthians 15, where Paul talks about the defeat of death. Knowing Jesus in our day-to-day lives here and now is wonderful, but it's not enough. If death is the end, than the enemy eventually wins. "If in this life only we have hope in Christ, we are of all men most miserable." (1 Cor. 15:19). But thank God it's not the end! Jesus is alive. The tomb where He laid is empty. And because He lives, we will live also (John 14:19).

The thing we can place our unshakable faith in is the defeat of death, of which Jesus's resurrection is proof. "When this corruptible will have put on incorruption, and this mortal will have put on immortality, then the saying that is written shall come to pass: 'Death is swallowed up in victory. O death, where is your sting? O grave, where is your victory?'" (1 Cor. 15:54–55). You can bet your life on the fact that the monster in the closet is soon to evaporate. There's no need to fear that which is already defeated.

If fear of death—your own or that of someone close to you— is still holding you in bondage, there is hope. I can tell you from my own experience that death hurts—a lot. It's an aberration in God's plan and proof that things are not all as God originally planned. It's an enemy worth raging and fighting against. But I can also tell you that the way out of the fear of death is through hope in the Resurrection. We do not have to feel sorrow over death or fear it in the same way as those who do not know the end of the story. (See 1 Thessalonians 4:13.)

Wrestling with grief and pain and loss is part of living in a broken, sinful, messed-up world. Knowing the absolute certainty of the Resurrection does not remove pain now, but it makes endurance possible. It's the guaranteed outcome that gives us the faith necessary to survive and overcome even during the very moments when we struggle with our wounds.

If you're not sure where you will go at the time of your own death, take care of that right now. The Bible says, "If you confess with your mouth Jesus is Lord, and believe in your heart that God has raised Him from the dead, you will be saved" (Rom. 10:9). It's as simple and profound as that.

> *Jesus, I need You. I believe You died for my sins, that You rose again, and that You are alive forever. I confess You as my Lord and Savior. Thank You for saving, healing, and restoring me, and making me alive with You forever. Amen.*

If you are certain of where you will go for eternity but the fear of death still holds you, first take stock of anything that is within your power to do that would lengthen and improve your life, such as optimizing your physical lifestyle, controlling your thoughts, managing stress well, and investing in healthy personal relationships. Then spend some time reading about how Jesus dealt with death and what the Bible says about the defeat of death. Read about how Jesus responded to the death of His friend Lazarus and what He said about death, life, and resurrection in John 11. Read Paul's treatise on death and resurrection in 1 Corinthians 15. Read his description of Christ's second coming in 1 Thessalonians 4:13–18.

A group of seminary students enjoyed getting together to play basketball in the gym as a way to decompress from their studies. The school janitor, an elderly man, would often sit reading his Bible while he waited for them to finish their game before locking up each evening. One night the students asked him, "What are you reading?"

"The Book of Revelation," the janitor responded.

"How can you understand what it means?" the students asked. "We have a hard time understanding Revelation even with all our education."

The janitor was undeterred. "Oh, I know what it means. It means that Jesus is going to win!"

Indeed, Jesus is going to win! Of that we can be absolutely certain. Death couldn't hold Him in the grave, and it won't be able to hold you either as long as you're on God's side. One of the sweetest promises in the Bible is this: "'God shall wipe away all tears from their eyes. There shall be no more death.' Neither shall there be any more sorrow nor crying nor pain, for the former things have passed away" (Rev. 21:4).

If all we have is this life, the fear of death would be enough to hold us captive. But thank God there is more. Fill your heart with Jesus's defeat of death in His resurrection and His assurance that you too can live. Let His presence grow your faith in the eventual outcome of this war, and your fear will disappear as surely as the monsters in the closet.

Let Revelation 22:20 be your prayer: "Even so, come Lord Jesus!"

OVERCOMING FEAR OF DEATH

Fear, and most specifically the fear of death, is one of the enemy's strongest weapons against us. As we experience Christ's victory, however, our freedom from fear makes us invincible to Satan's attacks. We come to the place where we know that we have won, even if we get wounded in the battle. Regardless of what happens during the remainder of our earthly lives, the devil has tried his best with us—and he has lost.

Coming to that place of victory is a process. Smaller battles prepare us for larger ones. Refuse to accept defeat in the smaller challenges you face, and use them as a means to develop your perspective, thinking, prayer life, and character. Faith in a guaranteed victory does not eliminate pain now, but it makes it possible to endure and even to thrive in the meantime. Fear of death will leave as you allow Christ's defeat of death, His resurrection, and His promise of eternal life to fill your heart.

Dear Lord, the fear of death still holds me. My grief over loved ones who have died feels too much. My battle right now feels overwhelming. I desperately need You—Your presence and Your victory.

Even through my loss or pain or fear, I choose faith. I believe You died and rose again and are alive forevermore. I believe Your resurrection defeated death and that death has no hold on me as Your follower. I believe You are coming again and that I along with all those who believe in You will live forever also. Death will die, and Your kingdom will never end. All my tears will be wiped away. Regardless of what happens during the remainder of my life here, I am completely certain of my eternal life with You.

Right now I claim Your victory over death as my own. The enemy has no hold on me—through death or any other means. Your blood covering me makes me secure in You. I claim the freedom from fear that Your victory makes available to me. I recognize Your presence as stronger than death—now and forever. Amen.

QUESTIONS FOR CONTEMPLATION AND DISCUSSION

1. What role does the fear of death play in your own struggle? Are you wrestling with grief over a loved one's death or fear of your own?

2. "The enemy has tried his best with you, and he has lost." Talk about what that means for you.

3. How certain are you of the Resurrection? What does Jesus's defeat of death and His promise of eternal life mean to you?

CHAPTER 14

STRATEGY FIVE: ENTER INTO WORSHIP

The Value of Being in God's Presence

THE PLACE OF safety—if you're a parent, your arms were that place for your child. When they got hurt, when they were sick, when there was a barking dog or too many new people or thunder or anything else that frightened them, they would raise their arms for you to pick them up or climb into your bed at night. Your presence could make monsters disappear and boo-boos feel all better, and little wounded spirits would be healed. If that was a long time ago, take a moment to remember what it felt like for your toddler to grab you around the neck and hold on for dear life when he or she was afraid or anxious.

That's what God's presence can do for you. In spiritual warfare the only place of safety is His arms, and worship is the way you get there.

We rightly call Satan's realm the kingdom of darkness. That's where fear and anxiety live, along with every other hurtful thing. And as you know, darkness does not leave a room or your life by trying to force it out; darkness leaves when you turn on the light. Jesus called Himself the light of the world (John 9:5). Where He is, darkness cannot exist. When He is there, the kingdom of darkness vanishes. When you are in His presence, darkness has no hold on you. "I have come as a light into the world, that whoever believes in Me should not remain in darkness" (John 12:46). Entering His presence is turning on the light.

There have probably been times when you experienced the presence of God in an unusually powerful way. We know He is with us always, but there are moments when our spiritual sensitivities are awakened and we become acutely aware of His presence. Our emotions can't live at that intensity continuously, even though we might wish to stay there. But you can be in His presence much more than you probably realize. You can be like the child who runs into the arms of their parent and finds comfort, safety, healing, peace, and so much more.

How we need that place of safety when we're facing spiritual warfare! That's what true worship will do for you.

HOW WORSHIP IMPACTS SPIRITUAL WARFARE

When you read through the Gospels, it becomes clear that Satan and his demons could not tolerate being in Jesus's presence. Jesus never backed down, and the demons had to leave. If a scene was created, it was the demons' doing, not Jesus's. He simply showed up, and anything evil had to go in the same way darkness leaves when light shows up.

It's that way in your life as well. If you feel distressed or tormented about entering the presence of God, it may be evidence that the enemy has a serious hold on you. It's time to ask for other spiritual warriors to pray for you, to confess anything you are aware of that may have allowed the devil into your life, and to plead the blood of Jesus. Your choice, even if it's difficult, to remain in God's presence will be the means of your deliverance. Stay in the presence of God long enough, and any demonic influence will have to go.

Hopefully you eagerly welcome being in the presence of God. The attacks of the enemy are far away at those moments, and his power in your life is broken. The fog lifts, your mind is quiet, and your soul is filled. To some degree you lose a sense of what's going on around you, and all you see is Jesus. As long as you're in that place, the enemy cannot touch you.

Sometimes the moments of being in the presence of God happen spontaneously. As in The Chronicles of Narnia, Aslan can show up any time He wants. Sometimes it's with a roar, sometimes it's with a voice calling our names, and sometimes it's with silence and is unseen. From our side the best and most consistent way to enter God's presence is through worship.

The difference between praise and worship

Much of contemporary Christian music is often called "praise and worship music." But praise and worship are really quite different. Praise is wonderful. We are told to praise the Lord: "It is good to sing praises unto our God; for it is pleasant, and a song of praise is fitting" (Ps. 147:1). The angels in heaven praise Him continually. Every time you read *Hallelujah* in Scripture it means "Praise the Lord."

Praise involves broadcasting how good and great God is, telling of the great things He has done for others and for you, expressing how He has conquered the kingdom of darkness, and proclaiming the good things He has promised to do for you and all His children. Praise has a role in spiritual warfare. Psalms says, "Let the high praises of God be in their mouths, and two-edged swords in their hands" (Ps. 149:6). Praise is part of telling the truth about God, and it presses back the forces of the enemy. It can raise your spirits and help you focus on God rather than your problems. There's nothing wrong with praise. Your spiritual life absolutely must include this vital dimension.

Worship, however, is more. Praise is telling people about God, while worship is always directed toward God Himself. Praise includes magnifying God for His mighty works and His love, while worship simply stands in awe of who He is. Praise is exuberant; worship stills your soul and everything in you. Praise can be solo or corporate; worship, even if done in the presence of others, is always a matter of your heart alone before God. Worship is the posture of this well-known verse: "Be still and know that I am God; I will be exalted among the nations, I will be exalted in the earth" (Ps. 46:10).

And it's in worship that He shows up.

When you truly see God as He is, you can't help but worship Him. On the Isle of Patmos John was visited by the glorified ascended Jesus. Words failed John as he tried to describe Him; eyes like flames of fire, a voice like many waters, shining as bright as the sun (Rev. 1:14–15). And John's response? It wasn't excitement or dancing or shouting or even joy. "When I saw Him, I fell at His feet as though I were dead" (v. 17). That's worship. Whether your body is kneeling or not, in worship your heart is prostrate and silent before Him. Your own words or actions simply don't fit. You're completely still in body and soul.

There is no greater place of safety from the enemy's attacks. You've run and thrown yourself into His arms, and nothing else can touch you there.

Cleansing and healing in worship

You cannot spend very long in God's presence and remain the same. Your fears and worries leave, of course, and all your earthly problems become so small. But there's more. The parts of you that need to be cleansed are washed clean. The parts of you that need to be transformed are changed. The parts of you that are broken become healed. "But we all, seeing the glory of the Lord with unveiled faces, as in a mirror, are being transformed into the same image from glory to glory by the Spirit of the Lord" (2 Cor. 3:18). Your body is often kneeling, your eyes are often closed, and your hands may be raised. But your spiritual eyes are wide open, totally transfixed on Him. And as His presence fills you through the eyes of your heart, your whole being is transformed.

You may try to white-knuckle it when trying to overcome fear, anxiety, or any other thought or behavior that does not line up with what God wants. I can almost feel your muscles tighten and see your fists clench. You've been hurt, and you're desperately trying to hold all the broken pieces of yourself together. You're desperately trying to look good, be good, and do good. How is this going for you? You're exhausted and feel hopeless.

You cannot become good by trying harder. You cannot heal yourself by plastering Band-Aids on your wounds. That would be like a pail of dirty water trying to clean itself up by tossing out the dirt drop by drop; it will never work. The only way to find cleansing and healing and transformation, the only hope of becoming clean and whole, is to spend time in God's presence— in that secret place of intimacy with God where the messed-up parts of you are transformed and knit together again as only He can do.

You cannot become good by trying harder. You can only be transformed by returning again and again to God's presence and letting Him change you.

Entering God's presence in worship involves being willing for Him to change you in the ways you can't change yourself. It may stretch you, and the changing may feel uncomfortable. But it is the only way in which you can become who He originally created you to be and who He has promised to transform you into. It's a place you want to be because of who He is and because of who you become as a result.

Submit to God, resist the devil.

Remember that this whole cosmic war is not about power or territory, but about allegiance. It's about who you will respect, honor, believe, follow, love, and worship. Even Jesus was faced with that exact temptation. When Satan tempted Jesus in the wilderness, he showed Jesus all the greatness of the world: "All these things I will give You if You will fall down and worship me" (Matt. 4:9). But Jesus made His allegiance to His Father clear: "Jesus said to him, 'Get away from here, Satan! For it is written, "You shall worship the Lord your God, and Him only shall you serve"'" (v. 10).

You too will have to choose who you will worship, and you will need to act on that choice repeatedly. When you consciously enter into worshipping God, you demonstrate on which side of the spiritual war you are standing. Even if you aren't thinking about spiritual warfare, your act of worship clearly places you on God's side. James said, "Submit yourselves to God. Resist the devil, and he will flee from you" (James 4:7). Is there any more complete way to submit to God than to worship Him? By your very act of doing so, you are resisting the devil, and he will flee.

Whoever has your attention has you. Whoever you continually spend time with, think about, look at, submit to, and admire has your allegiance. You will eventually become like the one you worship. That's the way God created human nature; you can't escape it. So if you want to become more like God, spend time with Him, looking at Him, admiring Him. If you are choosing to resist the devil and declare your allegiance for the God of heaven, worship Jesus. Worship is about forgetting yourself and filling your attention, your soul, your everything with Him.

HOW TO ENTER INTO WORSHIP

You may have sensed times of being in God's presence when you're with other believers in church or at some other Christian event. Those are awesome times, and God loves to show up when His people are gathered together. There is strength in numbers when it comes to spiritual warfare, so we need to gather regularly.

But there is also something very powerful about entering into worship yourself even when others aren't around. You don't have to wait until the next church service or Christian event to enter into God's presence and feel His power, safety, and healing. Many if not most of the enemy's attacks will come not when you're with other Christians but when you're alone. That's why it's important both to stay connected to other believers and to learn how to enter into God's presence any time you need to regardless of whether or not others are around you.

Whoever has your attention has you. You will
become like the one you worship and admire.

There are many spiritual practices that can be helpful in your Christian growth: Bible study, intercessory prayer, ministering to others in need, corporate praise. All of those are important. But what we're talking about here is worship. This does not negate the benefits of those other spiritual practices, but if you don't spend time tuning out every earthly thing—including yourself— and focusing your whole soul on God Himself, you will eventually run dry and become weak in spiritual warfare.

You may already know how to enter God's presence through worship. If so, treasure that and do more of it. If not, or if you need some other suggestions about entering into worship, here are several ways to do so. Remember that worship is focusing on God to the exclusion of everything else. It's a function of your inner spirit, not your intellect. It begins with a choice and then incorporates your emotions, your physical senses, your thoughts, and everything about you.

Worship with others

Not all Christian gatherings create a space where true worship can happen. Some do. Worship is not a song sung by a group of performers on stage, even though the music, lights, and entire atmosphere may be wonderful. Christian leaders who truly understand worship use these elements to create a space and time where you are able to worship, though these elements themselves are not worship.

Music that creates energy and excitement is praise, not worship. Inspirational Bible teaching helps you grow spiritually, but it is not worship. Sharing testimonies of what God has done in people's lives stimulates faith, but it is not worship. Joining with other believers in fellowship and love is a vital part of being in the body of Christ, but in itself it is not worship. An entire life of worship will include all those things, but there must be times when your soul is alone with God.

You will know that you have experienced worship when you lose interest in what is happening around you and all your focus is on God Himself. He is more present to you than the people around you or the music that is being played. You don't remember what you're wearing or what happened before you came. You don't care or even notice what anyone else may be thinking about you or what time it is. Your whole being is still.

Music sung to God by leaders who know how to tune in to God's presence can help you enter into worship, but it's still a choice you must make. You may feel an invitation in your heart to step into a place deeper than you're used to; listen to that invitation. You may close your eyes. You may lift your hands or kneel or bow your head or raise your eyes to the sky. Sometimes tears may come. What's going on around you fades as your senses focus on God's presence. It's more than a feeling, although wonderful feelings may wash over your soul. You're worshipping God, and He is all that matters.

Treasure the opportunities to join with other believers in true worship. If your church is not a place where this kind of worship is welcomed, check out other Christian gatherings, conferences, or events in addition to your home church. It will strengthen your walk with God and your effectiveness in spiritual warfare.

Worship with music by yourself

When facing some of my darkest moments, I learned to put on a CD of worship music that was especially meaningful to me and enter the presence of God right in my living room. You can do the same. Be selective in the music you choose. Remember that you're looking for music that quiets your soul and turns your focus to God and His presence. This is a great way to enter into worship any time you need to even when others aren't available. The music itself is not worship, but it's a great means to help you enter God's presence.

If you're struggling with fear or worry, it may take a little time for those feelings to subside. Turn on your worship music and let your soul discharge all the turmoil you're carrying. Cry or beg or scream for a bit if you must, but stay there long enough to let your soul become quiet so that you can enter God's presence. It's not that He isn't there in your tears, but He won't usually respond to your angst by adding His voice to the cacophony of sound in your mind. Cast all your worry onto Jesus, and then be still.

You wouldn't enter an earthly king's presence with a flurry of noise and activity, and it's very difficult to enter God's presence without being still. That may take some learning on your part. God is big enough to handle all your stuff—your pain, questions, anger, worries, and fears. But to get really close to Him, you need to leave them at the door when you enter His throne room. You must lose focus on your own stuff and turn yourself fully toward Him. That's where you abandon yourself and jump into His arms.

The most impactful times of solitary worship are when you are able to forget the clock and give God whatever time He chooses to take. But you don't have to wait for a day off or an evening alone to experience the benefits. You can turn on worship music while driving to work; tune out your own worries and fears, and focus on God's presence. You can forget your problems and enter into worship while mowing the lawn or making dinner. Use music as a tool, and then train your mind to turn its focus toward God regardless of your surroundings.

Listening prayer

As with conversations with your spouse or your best friend, there are many kinds of prayer—conversations with God. All of them are appropriate, but the kind of prayer that brings you fully into God's presence is worship. And worship is always still.

Elijah was running for his life, discouraged, and burned out. He ended up out in the wilderness at Mount Horeb where God met with him. There was a great wind, and then an earthquake, and then a fire, but God was not in any of those. Once everything was quiet, God showed up in a still, small voice, a "gentle whisper" (1 Kings 19:12, NIV). And Elijah's response? He covered his head in reverence, stood still, and listened (v. 13).

One of the best ways to use Scripture is to read a passage until a verse speaks something to your heart, then pause and let yourself just be there. It can be a way to enter into worshipful prayer. Or your heart may be so troubled that you can't focus on reading, and you just begin to pour out your distress to God. God's shoulders are big enough to carry it all. But again, stay there long enough to become quiet. Once you empty your heart to God, be still. Simply remain quiet and listen. Consciously choose to let your own stuff go, and turn your attention to Him.

Sometimes not much will happen, and that's OK. Sometimes your sense of God's presence will be brief and comforting, a moment of encouragement and strength. Sometimes He will show up more dramatically and His presence will linger as He heals your heart and speaks to you. As with any human relationship, every encounter is different, but the more you show up, the more His presence will mean to you. Each time you come, you will feel His presence more readily. Eventually you'll be able to sense His presence even when your feelings themselves aren't overwhelmed.

God's presence in nature

Human architecture, digital distractions, man-made noise of commerce or conversation or media—even at their best, they're no match for God's creation. Sometimes the best way to enter into worship is to go where God's best work is displayed. You've probably had times like that, when the rush of the ocean waves or the majesty of the mountains has reminded you that God is bigger than all your problems.

Spending time focused on God's creation in nature can be a wonderful way to enter His presence in worship. Again, the key is to quiet your own soul and turn your attention to Him. Nature can remind you of how much bigger He is than you and your problems, of His attention to detail, of His creativity and power, and of His extravagance and joy and love. You learn more about Him through observing the things He has made. It can help still your soul and put you in a place where you can hear Him.

Take a walk by the river or sit on the beach and let the waves wash through your soul. Go outside at night and look up at the stars—really look. Listen to His power in the lightning and thunder. Observe His glory in the sunrise or sunset. Even a tender flower or a bird's song can remind you of who is really in charge of all this. If He made and cares for the birds, won't He do the same for you? (See Matthew 6:26.)

Finding God's presence

When you're worried, confused, afraid, overwhelmed, or in pain, run into God's presence. Be like the child who runs into the parent's arms, grabs him or her around the neck, and holds on for dear life. Don't stay wallowing in your distress. There's no place of safety like God's presence. Nothing evil can touch you there.

And keep coming back again and again. All the other parts of the Bible are still true; we're on enemy territory, and in this world we will face trouble. But in His presence we can find true joy, true safety, true deliverance, and true transformation.

That's what worship will do for you.

WORSHIP GOD

God's presence is a place of safety from the attacks of the enemy. The kingdom of darkness cannot remain in God's presence. God can and will show up whenever He chooses, but the surest way to enter His presence is through worship. Worship is consciously turning away from everything else including your own problems and the activity of the enemy, and focusing entirely on God. Beyond praise, worship stills your soul, brings God's healing and transforming work into your life, and is a powerful way to resist the devil.

You can voluntarily enter into worship either with others or by yourself. In corporate settings be sensitive to the invitation in your heart to move deeper, forget your surroundings, and see God Himself. When alone you can also enter into worship through music that helps still your soul and focus on Him, through listening prayer, and by spending time with God's creation in nature.

> *Dear God, I choose to enter Your presence. You are greater than my problems. In Your presence the enemy has no power, and in Your presence I am safe from his attacks. I come to You as a child coming to a loving parent. I need Your protection, Your comfort, Your healing, Your cleansing, Your transformation. I need You!*
>
> *I choose to turn my focus away from everything else and look only to You. I bring all my fears, my worries, my hurts, my needs, my brokenness, and my battles, and I lay them down at the door of Your presence. I choose to quiet my soul of all the noise and commotion and be still in Your presence. I look away from myself and fix my eyes on You, on Your face.*
>
> *And now, as I am still in Your presence, please speak to me. Do in my heart what is needed. I am simply here, waiting on You. Amen.*

QUESTIONS FOR CONTEMPLATION AND DISCUSSION

1. When have you sensed God's presence in an extraordinary way? What was the setting? How were you different after that experience?

2. What does *worship* mean to you? Can you describe the essential quality of worship that differentiates it from praise or other spiritual practices?

3. Talk about what you can do this week to enter into God's presence through worship.

CHAPTER 15

STRATEGY SIX: WALK IN VICTORY

Consistently Applying Christ's Finished Work in Your Life

'M A PROFESSIONAL. In the work I do as a physician, I write prescriptions, deliver babies, perform surgeries, and give directions to other members of the health care team. I'm expected to provide consistent high-quality care to my patients using the best information and skills available to me. Those expectations are the same regardless of how I feel on any given day. I can't get away with performing a surgery less skillfully simply because I'm tired, upset about a nasty e-mail, or anxious to get to a birthday party for one of my grandchildren.

Writing prescriptions, doing surgery, and giving medical orders don't make me a doctor; if I tried to do those things without the appropriate training, experience, and credentials I'd be hauled off to jail. I do those things because I *am* a physician and because I *am* a professional. That's what professional doctors do. My behavior flows out of who I have become. I really don't have much choice in the matter. I'm either a doctor, or I'm not.

Do I do those things perfectly every time? Absolutely not. But I'm responsible for giving it my absolute best every single time I interact with a patient or other health care professional. I don't try to do it; I just do it. I'm also responsible for taking care of myself well enough so that I can do my best and for continuing to learn so that I remain at the forefront of my profession.

You are a professional too. If you're a believer, if you've

accepted Jesus as your Lord and Savior and have chosen to be a part of God's kingdom, you are a professional. You may not feel like one much of the time, but you are one. You don't get a free pass on days when you just don't feel like it. You probably don't do it "right" all the time, but you're either a Christian or you're not. This is what you signed up for when you said yes to Jesus.

It's just like marriage or pregnancy. You're either pregnant or you're not. You're either married or you're not. You can't be a little bit pregnant or a little bit married. And you can't be a little bit Christian either.

So what does it mean to be a Christian? Just as doctors write prescriptions, do surgery, and give medical orders, there are just some things Christians do. Some Christians are more experienced than others in some of these things, and some specialize in some areas more than others, but there are some things Christians do simply because they're Christians:

- Leave the old life of sin behind (Rom. 6:1–4).

- Grow to increasingly become more like Jesus (Rom. 8:29; 2 Cor. 3:18).

- Overcome Satan and the kingdom of darkness (Rev. 12:11).

- Walk in a new life of victory in Christ (Rom. 8:4; Eph. 5:8).

- Look forward to the final expression of the kingdom of God when He makes all things new (Heb. 12:1–2; Rev. 21:1).

There are some things you do simply because you are a Christian. Among those is to stand as an overcomer against the kingdom of darkness.

Christians don't do these things perfectly all the time. I sure don't, and neither will you. Doing these things doesn't make you a Christian; you do them because you are one. You do them because of who you are and who you are becoming.

This is an awesome privilege. Spiritual warfare is not about mustering up enough courage to stand up against the devil or frantically flinging around any spiritual weapon you can find to defeat an attack. Jesus simply was, and being who He was both stirred up the opposition and demonstrated His victory. You too simply are a believer. All the warfare—and most importantly the victory—flows from that.

So let's look at what that *being* a Christian looks like and how you can stand firm in this victory.

STANDING FIRM IN VICTORY

The word *stand* is an important one. When you think of spiritual warfare you may often think of Ephesians 6, where Paul talks about putting on the armor or God. Right at the beginning of that passage he talks about standing: "Therefore put on the full armor of God, so that when the day of evil comes, you may be able to *stand your ground*, and after you have done everything, to *stand*. *Stand firm* then…" (Eph. 6:13–14, NIV). The Greek verb used here is sometimes translated "to be." It signifies solidly holding one's ground, being placed firmly in one location, immovable, there for a purpose.[1] That's the place of victory.

You don't have to go out and do anything specific to prove you're an overcomer. When you became a believer, an overcomer was part of what you became (Rev. 12:11). In Christ you are a new creation; you share in His new resurrection life (2 Cor. 5:17). In Him you are a victorious overcomer; you share in His victory over evil. You simply come to realize that and take your stand. You don't go out and fight the devil in order to become an overcomer any more than I write a prescription in order to become a doctor; you overcome the devil because you are an overcomer.

I hope this truth burns into your soul like a permanent brand on cowhide. All the stuff you do as a Christian, especially the strategies of spiritual warfare we've talked about in this book, will become empty and ineffective if you simply try to employ them as techniques. If, on the other hand, you use them out of a deep conviction of who you are in Christ, of your new victorious nature as a believer, they will flow naturally and powerfully out of you as part of that river of living water Jesus promised (John 7:38).

In spiritual warfare this means you must first place your time and energy into being. Your Bible reading, your church attendance, your daily prayer, your connection with other believers, your speaking truth, your pleading the blood of Jesus—it's not directed outward so much as it is taking your stand and reinforcing your stand as part of God's kingdom. The outward techniques and strategies can look different over time and in different circumstances, but your stand as a believer never changes. When you invest in being a believer in this way you are engaging in spiritual warfare.

This also means that you don't accept defeat. Whenever your mind wants to focus on your problems, you simply bring it back to standing in Christ's victory. Whenever something happens that feels like defeat—an illness, a financial setback, an overwhelming negative emotion, a sin—you refuse to allow that to define who you are. Instead, look at the circumstances honestly (the Stockdale paradox again) and then turn your attention back to your leader, Jesus, in whose victory you stand.

Your definition of victory won't be the same as what the world would describe as victory. You're not lording it over other people; you're serving them. It's possible that you may continue to experience emotional, physical, material, or relational challenges; it's the cross fire we get from living in this sinful world until the time when Jesus returns. But none of these things move you (Acts 20:24). You simply stand where you are as an overcomer, confident in the eventual outcome of victory.

There will be things you do as a result of this kind of being. Standing is not passive. You're on a mission here, and that will involve spiritual disciplines to remain strongly connected to God and to His people, acting out Jesus's love to those He sends you to and pressing back the kingdom of darkness through speaking in Jesus's name when confronted with evil. That will all come from the inside, from a heart that is being transformed as a result of spending time in God's presence. Your spiritual behaviors come from who you are on the inside.

FILLING THE EMPTY PLACES

"Nature abhors a vacuum" is not only a cliché; it's true, both in nature and your life. When something leaves your life, something else will take its place. That's true of your thoughts, your time, your attention, and your relationships. When the thing that leaves was taking up a big part of your life, such as going to school, raising children, a career, or a marriage, it can feel very uncomfortable until that place in your life has been filled up again. That's one big reason why divorce, retirement, or even an empty nest are often so traumatic.

> What would your life look like if you were no longer afraid—of anything? What would you do with your life if you were no longer anxious? Why not start living that way today?

When something unhealthy, ungodly, or even evil leaves your life, you may feel a tremendous sense of relief. Your fear is gone. You no longer wallow in anxiety. Your chains are broken, and you're breathing free. Hallelujah! But that space in your life must be filled up again, or others—including the enemy—will fill it for you. Jesus talked about what happens when an evil spirit leaves a person's life. If the space occupied by that spirit is left empty, the enemy will return and fill it with even more evil spirits, and "the last state of that man is worse than the first" (Matt. 12:45).

You need to be intentional about filling up the space in your life that fear, anxiety, or anything else that is ungodly was occupying. You have a very important choice here about what your life will look like going forward. When you've been accustomed to being a slave, it may take some time and effort to learn how to live free. You may have detested your fear, anxiety, and psychological or other distress, but it was all you knew. It became somewhat comfortable. You could blame it for how you spent your time, for your inability to give others what they needed, and for your failure to accomplish anything significant for the kingdom of God. But it is gone now, and it's time to choose what you will replace it with.

What if you were no longer afraid—of anything? How would your mind look at problems? What would you think about? How would you relate to people who may not particularly like you? What risks would you take in relationships, business, or ministry? What might you begin to do in accomplishing the mission God gave you as best as you understand it?

What if you were no longer anxious? What would your mind focus on, ruminate about, or imagine? How would your day be different—in how you spent your time or in what going to bed at night felt like? What kind of extra energy would you have, and how would you invest it? What activities would you engage in for the benefit of others?

God has not only set you free *from* bondage to fear and anxiety and everything else the enemy would bring against you; He has also set you free *for* something. God did not create you and me to simply exist in our own comfort and for our own pleasure. There's something bigger for which He created you and for which He has set you free. "For we are His workmanship, created in Christ Jesus for good works, which God prepared beforehand" (Eph. 2:10).

What is it that your fear or anxiety or any other bondage was keeping you from doing? What piece do you know right now of the purpose for which God put you on this planet? You may feel as though you don't know much at all about what that purpose is. Start moving forward in small steps in any area you do know. As you do, God will make more of your purpose clear to you. He doesn't lay out the whole journey ahead of you all at once; He usually gives you some small steps to take, and as you are obedient in following Him in small things, He will make more clear to you.

God has not only set you free from bondage to
the kingdom of darkness. He has also set you free
for something. Start moving into that now.

Don't make the mistake of thinking God's purpose for you is limited to something big or something separate from your personality, skills, and passions. Simply start where you are, perhaps with something like these:

- Give a smile or a hug to someone you notice who is hurting.

- Be present—truly present—with your children.

- Share your story of overcoming with someone who is facing a similar struggle as you have.

- Write an encouraging Facebook post about something God has done for you.

- Volunteer for a larger challenge at work, and give it your very best.

- Notice someone who is interested in what you can teach them—a coworker, a teen, or someone without a job—and pour yourself into them.

- Create a product that helps people, and go sell it.

God will give you opportunities to use what He has given you—in your family, in your church, in your vocation, or in your world. Just step forward and begin giving of yourself. Your purpose is not so much something God drops on you in one dramatic moment; it's more something you discover and develop as you and God work through stuff together. And it's always connected with someone or some cause that's bigger than yourself. It may be your own family; it may be your coworkers, students, employees, or church family; or it may be a larger group whose pain you feel.

WHEN YOU FEEL AS THOUGH YOU'VE FAILED AGAIN

It would be nice if your victory over fear, anxiety, or any of the enemy's attacks was a one-time thing and you never had to face those challenges again. But things don't usually work out that way. There's enough going on in our sinful world to cause you to be anxious and afraid most of the time. Your physical body's vulnerabilities, your mental habits, your personality, the battle scars you carry from spiritual warfare—they can all seemingly haunt you especially when you're tired or alone. And the enemy is only too happy to come at you with more attacks if he thinks there's any chance of success—or simply to harass you.

You will almost certainly have times in the future when you feel as though you've failed again. You will feel a moment of fear or anxiety and wonder if all your victory was just a sham. You'll be tempted to question whether you've actually won any real spiritual battles and whether it's even worth hoping for victory at all.

Don't believe those lies. Sometimes your mind will try to dismiss how far you've come because the present challenge seems so overwhelming. Sometimes the enemy will do all he can to get you to move your focus away from Christ's victory and onto your own vulnerabilities and "failures." You will be tempted to do anything else but stand. But those thoughts—either from your own head or from the enemy—are just lies. That's when you need to stand more than ever. That's when you pull out the strategies you've learned about spiritual warfare and use them all over again.

You have not failed just because you have some momentary feelings that are similar to what was holding you in bondage in the past. You now have the choice about how you respond to those feelings. Yes, you could admit defeat, crawl back into your prison, and sit there feeling sorry for yourself, thinking "All this spiritual warfare stuff doesn't work. I'm hopeless." Or you can refuse to let negative thoughts and feelings take control of you.

You can choose to remember the freedom you have come to in Christ and focus on doing the next right thing.

Here are some quick questions to help you assess what may be going on when you feel attacked and once again need to take your stand in Christ's victory:

- Is there any place where I have allowed the enemy entry into my life recently?

- What thoughts and feelings are going on in my head? Are they based on the enemy's lies or on reality—including what God has to say?

- Am I doing all I can to stay connected to other believers in a healthy way?

- What truth can I speak right now? What do I need to plead the blood of Jesus over right now?

- What am I afraid of? What does God have to say about that fear?

- Have I run into God's presence recently in worship? How can I do that right now?

Running through those questions doesn't have to take a lot of time. You can do it in a few minutes, certainly during a quiet time with the Lord in the morning or before bed. Just the habit of doing so may well get you back on track, and it will certainly help you see what area you may need to focus on next. Praying in the Spirit at those times is a great way to connect your spirit with heaven once again. Feeling like a failure doesn't mean you have lost; that's exactly the time to move beyond your feelings and take your stand in being part of Christ's victory.

THE BEST EVIDENCE FOR GOD'S KINGDOM

You yourself are a weapon. You by your very existence as an overcomer in Christ are a weapon of spiritual warfare. Aside from Jesus's death and resurrection, your very decision to be part of the kingdom of God instead of the kingdom of darkness is the most important defeat of the enemy. In this battle for your allegiance your stand on God's side is evidence that Jesus has won.

And the longer you remain in God's kingdom and the more resolutely you stand, the stronger that evidence becomes. The more your character becomes like Christ's, the more you refuse to believe the enemy's lies or allow his attacks to take you down, and the more you allow the Holy Spirit to transform every part of you—spirit, soul, and body—into who God created you to be, the more effective you become as an agent in demonstrating the truth of Jesus's victory over evil.

Who you are as a believer, who you become as an overcomer in Christ, is the best evidence of all that God exists, that He is who He said He is, that Satan is defeated, and that Jesus has won. You, as a transformed re-created victorious follower of Jesus, are also the most effective advertisement for the kingdom of God. Others will see you and believe that God can do the same for them. Your living as an overcomer will help others become overcomers, and that will expand the kingdom of God and help others come out of the kingdom of darkness. That's when you become exceptionally dangerous to the enemy.

You—by your very existence as an overcoming
believer being transformed into Christ's likeness—
are the best evidence that God exists, that He
is who He says He is, and that He has been
victorious over the kingdom of darkness.

"For freedom Christ freed us. Stand fast therefore and do not be entangled again with the yoke of bondage" (Gal. 5:1). Jesus has won complete victory over evil. Will you take the victory He has offered you as your own? Will you stand firm in that victory as a believer?

Others are watching. The universe is watching. God needs you. We need you. Don't let us down!

LIVE IN VICTORY

Overcoming fear and anxiety and anything else from the enemy is not a one-time event. As a follower of Jesus you are an overcomer. Part of your new nature as a believer is that you stand against the enemy in whatever he brings against you. Future attacks do not mean failure; you can meet them with the same assurance of victory.

Jesus has not only set you free *from* evil; He has also set you free *for* a specific purpose. As you experience freedom from fear and anxiety, you will need to fill the places those things had in your life by actively moving toward the purpose God has for you. As you take small steps forward, God will make further steps clear to you.

Your existence as an overcoming believer who is becoming transformed into the likeness of Jesus is the best evidence of—and advertisement for—the kingdom of God.

> *Dear Lord, I choose to stand firm in the freedom You have made available to me. I refuse to accept defeat in any of the enemy's attacks against me, knowing that You have given me everything I need to live in victory. When I am tempted to believe my feelings or outward circumstances that look like defeat, I choose to believe that as Your follower I am an overcomer. I accept all the victorious life You have for me here and now, and I look forward to the final victory when evil will be forever eliminated when You make all things new.*
>
> *I believe You have set me free for a purpose. I choose to step forward in that purpose as best as I understand it and ask that You make the next steps clear to me. I choose to keep my focus on You. I thank You for the life You have made available to me and that You call me to. I am part of Your kingdom forever. Amen.*

QUESTIONS FOR CONTEMPLATION AND DISCUSSION

1. What does the concept of a "professional" say about being a Christian? What does a Christian do simply because of who they are and who they are becoming?

2. Fear, anxiety, or other distress occupied a place in your life. What are you going to fill that place up with now?

3. What habits are you going to incorporate into your daily spiritual life that will help you stand firm against anything the enemy would bring?

4. What kind of an advertisement for the kingdom of God do you want to be?

NOTES

ACKNOWLEDGMENTS

1. Carol Peters-Tanksley, "Decreasing Anxiety Through Training in Spiritual Warfare" (Doctor of Ministry Dissertation, Oral Roberts University, 2009).

INTRODUCTION

1. Jim Stockdale and Sybil Stockdale, *In Love & War* (New York: Harper & Row, 1984); "Vice Admiral James B. Stockdale," United States Naval Academy, accessed December 19, 2016, https://www.usna.edu/Ethics/bios/stockdale.php.

2. Jim Collins, *Good to Great* (New York: HarperCollins, 2011), 85.

3. Ibid.

4. Ibid.

5. Ibid., 86.

CHAPTER 1 | WHAT'S WRONG WITH ME?

1. Kurt Kroenke et al., "Anxiety Disorders in Primary Care: Prevalence, Impairment, Comorbidity, and Detection," *Annals of Internal Medicine* 146, no. 5 (March 2007): 317–325.

2. Ronald C. Kessler et al., "Prevalence, Severity, and Comorbidity of Twelve-Month DSM-IV Disorders in the National Comorbidity Survey Replication (NCS-R)," *Archives of General Psychiatry* 62, no. 6 (June 2005): 617–627.

3. Anita Soni, "Anxiety and Mood Disorders: Use and Expenditures for Adults 18 and Older, U.S. Civilian Noninstitutionalized Population, 2007," Statistical Brief #303, Agency for Healthcare Research and Quality, December 2010,

accessed January 12, 2017, https://meps.ahrq.gov/data_files/publications/st303/stat303.pdf.

4. Fred J. Hanna and Martin H. Ritchie, "Seeking the Active Ingredients of Psychotherapeutic Change: Within and Outside the Context of Therapy," *Professional Psychology: Research and Practice* 26, no. 2 (April 1995): 180.

CHAPTER 2 | PHYSICAL CAUSES OF FEAR AND ANXIETY

1. Hans Selye, "Stress and the General Adaptation Syndrome," *British Medical Journal* 1, no. 4667 (June 1950): 1383–1392.

2. M. A. Waszczuk, H. M. S. Zavos, and T. C. Eley, "Genetic and Environmental Influences on Relationship Between Anxiety Sensitivity and Anxiety Subscales in Children," *Journal of Anxiety Disorders* 27, no. 5 (June 2013): 475–484.

3. James A. Blumenthal and Patrick J. Smith, "Risk Factors: Anxiety and Risk of Cardiac Events," *Nature Reviews Cardiology* 7, no. 11 (November 2010): 606–608.

4. "Statistics About Diabetes," American Diabetes Association, updated December 12, 2016, accessed December 19, 2016, http://www.diabetes.org/diabetes-basics/statistics/?referrer=https://www.google.com/.

CHAPTER 3 | DIFFICULT CIRCUMSTANCES CAUSING FEAR AND ANXIETY

1. Adriana Feder et al., "Posttraumatic Growth in Former Vietnam Prisoners of War," *Psychiatry* 71, no. 4 (2008): 359–370.

2. Jeremy Loudenback, "The 'Silent Epidemic' of Child Trauma," *The Chronicle of Social Change*, March 24, 2016, accessed December 19, 2016, https://chronicleofsocialchange.org/los-angeles/child-trauma-as-a-silent-epidemic/16869.

3. R. Takizawa, B. Maughan, and L. Arseneauly, "Adult Health Outcomes of Childhood Bullying Victimization:

Evidence From a Five-Decade Longitudinal British Birth Cohort," *American Journal of Psychiatry* 171, no. 7 (July 2014): 777–784.

4. Find more info and a group near you at www.griefshare.org.

5. For a representative summary, see Gene G. Ano and Erin B. Vasconcelles, "Religious Coping and Psychological Adjustment to Stress: A Meta-Analysis," *Journal of Clinical Psychology* 61, no. 4 (April 2005): 461–480.

CHAPTER 4 | THE ROLE OF YOUR MIND

1. Find more info at www.celebraterecovery.com.

CHAPTER 5 | THE ROLE OF YOUR LIFESTYLE

1. Find out the glycemic index of individual foods at www .glycemicindex.com.

2. Find more information at www.juiceplus.com.

3. "American Psychological Association Survey Shows Money Stress Weighing on Americans' Health Nationwide," American Psychological Association, Press Release, February 4, 2015, accessed January 13, 2017, http://www.apa.org/news/ press/releases/2015/02/money-stress.aspx.

4. Go to www.crown.org for more information on Crown Financial Ministries and www.daveramsey.com/fpu for more information on Financial Peace University.

CHAPTER 7 | "BE ANXIOUS FOR NOTHING"

1. Kenneth Pargament et al., "Religion and the Problem-Solving Process: Three Styles of Coping," *Journal for the Scientific Study of Religion* 27, no. 1 (March 1988), 99.

2. Blue Letter Bible, s.v. *"epiriptō,"* accessed February 9, 2017, https://www.blueletterbible.org/lang/lexicon/lexicon .cfm?Strongs=G1977&t=KJV.

CHAPTER 8 | "BE NOT AFRAID"

1. Etta B. Degering, *My Bible Friends Book Two* (Mountain View, CA: Pacific Press Publishing Association, 1977).

2. *American Heritage Dictionary of the English Language, Fifth Edition*, s.v. "strong nuclear force," accessed January 13, 2017, http://www.thefreedictionary.com/strong+nuclear+force.

3. N. R. Silton et al. "Beliefs About God and Mental Health Among American Adults," *Journal of Religion and Health* 53, no. 5 (October 2014); 1285–1296.

4. M. Song and E. Giovannucci, "Preventable Incidence and Mortality of Carcinoma Associated With Lifestyle Factors Among White Adults in the United States," *JAMA Oncology* 2, no. 9 (September 2016): 1154–1161.

5. Go to www.toastmasters.org for more information.

CHAPTER 9 | HOW JESUS DEALT WITH EVIL

1. Flavius Josephus, *Antiquities of the Jews*, book 8, chapter 2, accessed February 9, 2017, http://www.biblestudytools.com/history/flavius-josephus/antiquities-jews/book-8/chapter-2.html.

2. C. S. Lewis, *The Screwtape Letters*, (New York: HarperOne, 2015), ix.

3. Peters-Tanksley, "Decreasing Anxiety Through Training in Spiritual Warfare."

4. "A Mighty Fortress Is Our God" by Martin Luther, trans. by Frederick H. Hedge, 1853. Public domain.

5. Gregory Boyd, *God at War: The Bible & Spiritual Conflict* (Downers Grove, IL: Inter-Varsity, 1997), 186, emphasis in original.

6. Blue Letter Bible, s.v. *"exousia,"* accessed February 9, 2017, https://www.blueletterbible.org/lang/lexicon/lexicon .cfm?Strongs=G1849&t=KJV.

CHAPTER 10 | STRATEGY ONE: GUARD YOUR HEART

1. "The 9/11 Commission Report: Executive Summary," National Commission on Terrorist Attacks Upon the United States, August 2004, accessed December 22, 2016, http:// govinfo.library.unt.edu/911/report/911Report_Exec.htm.

2. B. A. Larsen et al., "The Immediate and Delayed Cardio-vascular Benefits of Forgiving," *Psychosomatic Medicine* 74, no. 7 (July 20, 2012): 745–750.

3. L. L. Toussaint, A. D. Owen, A. Cheadle, "Forgive to Live: Forgiveness, Health, and Longevity," *Journal of Behavioral Medicine* 35, no. 4 (August 2012): 375–386.

4. G. L. Reed and R. D. Enright, "The Effects of Forgiveness Therapy on Depression, Anxiety, and Posttraumatic Stress for Women After Spousal Emotional Abuse," *Journal of Consulting and Clinical Psychology* 74, no. 5 (2006): 920–929.

5. Corrie ten Boom, "I'm Still Learning to Forgive," *Guidepost*, November 1972.

CHAPTER 11 | STRATEGY TWO: STAY CONNECTED

1. Kenneth Pargament et al., "Patterns of Positive and Nega-tive Religious Coping With Major Life Stressors," *Journal for the Scientific Study of Religion* 37, no. 4 (April 1998): 710–724.

2. Go to www.celebraterecovery.com for more information.

CHAPTER 12 | STRATEGY THREE: SPEAK UP!

1. Colin MacLeod et al., "The Production Effect: Delinea-tion of a Phenomenon," *Journal of Experimental Psychology:*

Learning, Memory, and Cognition 36, no. 3 (May 2010): 671–685.

CHAPTER 13 | STRATEGY FOUR: HAVE NO FEAR

1. Tertullian, *Apologeticus*, chapter 50.

CHAPTER 15 | STRATEGY SIX: WALK IN VICTORY

1. Frederick Danger, ed., *A Greek-English Lexicon of the New Testament and Other Early Christian Literature, Third Edition* (Chicago IL: University of Chicago Press, 2000), 482.

DR. CAROL WOULD LOVE TO HEAR FROM YOU!

———o———

You can write to her at *drcarolministries.com*.
Join Dr. Carol on her website/blog for many more resources:
www.drcarolministries.com

ABOUT DR. CAROL

———o———

Carol Peters-Tanksley, MD, DMin (sometimes known to her friends as "Doctor-Doctor") is a licensed ob-gyn and also a doctor of ministry. She has practiced medicine for over twenty-five years and is board certified in obstetrics-gynecology and reproductive endocrinology. She currently practices part time so as to devote more time to writing and other ministry efforts.

While continuing to practice medicine, she sought ministry training and completed a DMin degree from Oral Roberts University. She subsequently founded Totally Free Ministries (now Dr. Carol Ministries) as a nonprofit Christian ministry dedicated to helping people discover the Fully Alive kind of life that Jesus came to give each one of us.

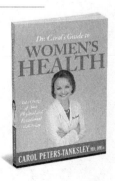

Dr. Carol and her husband, Al Tanksley, cohosted the *Dr. Carol Show* radio program for over five years until shortly before his death in 2016. Dr. Carol also enjoys speaking to church groups, women's groups, and doctors in training, among others.

Dr. Carol makes her home in Austin, Texas, where she enjoys being Grandma Carol to four wonderful grandchildren.

———————

ALSO BY DR. CAROL

———o———

Dr. Carol's Guide to Women's Health: Take Charge of Your Physical and Emotional Well-Being brings together medical science, the author's practical experience, and a faith perspective to the full spectrum of physical and mental health issues women face throughout the various seasons of their lives.

A healthy woman is so much more than her reproductive organs!

 DrCarolT   @DrCarolTanksley

CONNECT WITH US!

CHARISMA
HOUSE

(Spiritual Growth)

Facebook.com/CharismaHouse

@CharismaHouse

Instagram.com/CharismaHouse

(Health)

Pinterest.com/CharismaHouse

MODERN
ENGLISH
VERSION

(Bible)
www.mevbible.com

Ignite Your SPIRITUAL HEALTH
with these FREE Newsletters

CHARISMA HEALTH
Get information and news on health-related topics and studies, and tips for healthy living.

POWER UP! FOR WOMEN
Receive encouraging teachings that will empower you for a Spirit-filled life.

CHARISMA MAGAZINE NEWSLETTER
Get top-trending articles, Christian teachings, entertainment reviews, videos and more.

CHARISMA NEWS WEEKLY
Get the latest breaking news from an evangelical perspective every Monday.

SIGN UP AT:
nl.charismamag.com

CHARISMA MEDIA